THE ART OF WINNING WARS

THE ART OF
WINNING WARS

Colonel James Mrazek

U.S.A., Ret.

WALKER AND COMPANY

NEW YORK

First published in the United States of America in 1968 by Walker and Company, a division of the Walker Publishing Company, Inc.

Published simultaneously in Canada by The Ryerson Press, Toronto.

Library of Congress Catalog Card Number: 68-27376

ACKNOWLEDGMENTS AND COPYRIGHTS

The author wishes to express his gratitude for permission to quote from the following material:

The Army Quarterly and Defence Journal for material that already has appeared in that journal.

Office of the Chief of Military History, United States Army, Washington, D.C., "The Command Decision" by Lothar Rendulic.

Prentice-Hall, Inc., *Sea Power: A Naval History,* edited by E. B. Potter and Chester W. Nimitz. Copyright © 1960 by Prentice-Hall, Inc., Engle-wood Cliffs, New Jersey.

Scientific American, "The Psychology of Imagination," by Frank Barron. Copyright © 1958 by Scientific American, Inc. All rights reserved.

Simon & Schuster, Inc., *The Story of Civilization, Part II, The Life of Greece* by Will Durant. Copyright © 1939 by Will Durant.

Simon & Schuster, Inc., *The Story of Civilization, Part III, Caesar and Christ* by Will Durant. Copyright © 1944 by Will Durant.

Printed in the United States of America.

Book designed by Paula Wiener

355
M93

Contents

9/268

CHAPTER ONE

The Issue—
National Survival

There are few men among them who knew our *minds*,
and how we were fighting. If there had been more, we
would not have won the war so easily.

MAO TSE-TUNG

THE UNITED STATES OF AMERICA is defended by the strongest
military force ever assembled by man. Has it not emerged
victorious (or at least undefeated) from every conflict in
its short history? Can it not, at will, incinerate the known
world? Would it not be the rankest heresy to suggest that
this behemoth could (and may yet) be brought low, not by
an equally armed mammoth, but by a ragtag and bobtail
crew using a weapon scornfully credited to painters and
sculptors? I propose to commit this heresy, and in this book
I present proof that it is not heresy at all but a sober
statement of possibility.

The weapon, readily available to all men, inexhaustible
in volume and used lavishly, even now, to sell TV dinners
and political personalities, is creativity, that innate quality
of man that drives him to seek a better way of doing things.

At first it seems strange to think of creativity in the context

1

of battle. But most significant military victories have been artistic masterpieces, owing more to insight than infantry. They are the result of an innovative idea emanating from the mind of a creative leader. The military might, formerly so often regarded as the sole cause of victory, is frequently only the midwife, as it were, assisting in the birth of a victory which has already been conceived. From a creative point of view, battlefield successes often compare in emotional impact and, incongruously, in a kind of beauty with the paintings of a Rembrandt or the vibrant symphonies of a Tchaikovsky.

A creative victory may be vast enough to change the course of history, as when Alexander the Great defeated Darius. Or it may be a minor affair, a bitter encounter in a Vietnamese jungle defile. An innovative tactic had to be created for the particular circumstance; each was the product of the mind, usually of a single mind.

Repeatedly in warfare, new creative ideas and intuitions have provided history's foremost military leaders with the means to strike an annihilating blow. In spite of this fact, Western military leaders, with few notable exceptions, fail to see war as an aesthetic exercise and, consequently, ignore creativity's vital role in it. There are leaders in the world today who have a different view, and we face them, even now, on the bloodstained battlefield of Viet Nam.

From the Chinese Communist faith in creativity has evolved Lin Piao's manifesto[1]. It is the vast program for world conquest formulated by Mao Tse-tung's second-in-command and published September 2, 1965. Scholars equate Piao's forbidding document with Karl Marx's *Manifesto,* Hitler's *Mein Kampf,* and Nasser's *A Philosophy of Revolution.* In strident phrases, Marshal Lin Piao outlines Peking's intentions in Asia, its plans for the expansion of the Chinese variety of Communism. Moreover, he forecasts who will carry the banners and how the bearers will win. The manifesto makes clear that power will come from the peasants and will be wielded in its early stages by guerrillas who will topple city-based political power centers.

Lin Piao states only as much as he cares to reveal. What he has purposely left unsaid relates to the use of creativity in warfare and is a crucial matter to those who would try to understand how Communist China feels it can succeed in its strategy. Only when aware of what the Chinese are not revealing will one be able to understand why Lin Piao, his generals, and his servants in Viet Nam can courageously and confidently embark on their incredible course of world conquest while boldly confronted by the mightiest nation the world has ever seen and faced by the threat of nuclear incineration.

At the core of the Communist resolve lies faith in the creativity of men, for it is from intellect that ideas will flow that will protect and improve their society. Consequently, ideas rank foremost in Mao's arsenals. His followers appear to have grasped the essence and the broad social and political importance of creativity, in particular the overriding significance of this intellectual gift as a means of obtaining success on the battlefield. Adequate testimony to this is the Viet Cong guerrillas' record of combat successes, which competent military authorities attribute to surprise lethal devices and upsetting tactical ingenuity.

Few people recognize the fact that the manifesto merely extends to the realm of war Mao Tse-tung's confidence in the creative genius of the common man. He has said ". . . there is a great creative power among the people and there are thousands of geniuses among them. There are geniuses in every village, every town, every city."[2]

I believe that when Mao made that statement in 1943

there were few American politicians and no American military leaders remotely aware af creativity's vital role to a people's welfare. Today politicians and national and local officials are becoming more and more aware of its relationship to the outbreak of violence in our cities. Intellectual creativity and its processes and products are finally attracting long-deserved attention. Once the province of a few inquisitive artists and philosophers, the creative phenomena are now being studied both here and abroad by a proliferation of research groups. Curiously, the United States military services have almost wholly neglected to follow these trends.

The services appear to be alone among the professions in failing to realize that they too may find that creativity may benefit them. They are sadly deficient in their knowledge of the subject and wholly lacking in any understanding of how to make creativity pay off, not only in combat but also in staff planning, in research and development of weapons systems, and in doctrinal development.

What few efforts the military services have made in this direction have been halfhearted, narrowly conceived, and short-term and have not been adequately tied in to the critical problems of the battlefield. The projects have tended to go off on tangents and too often have not exploited the growing core of source data being made available by competent research in business, industry, and education.

The Army, notably in its Command Management School at Fort Belvoir, Virginia, has taken some effective measures to encourage creativity among selected key staff and command personnel. Its creativity instruction has been well received by them and has contributed toward making the subject more generally understood by these fortunate few. But the courses are geared solely to management and not to combat needs.

In other fields, the Army has been grossly negligent, making no broad use of creativity. It needs to do much more, as do the other services. The Air Force, for instance, though a service pioneer, starting investigation into creativity shortly after World War II, in recent years appears to have lost interest and for all practical purposes its work in this area has lapsed. West Point, Annapolis, and the Air Force Academy give the subject only passing attention. These institutions apparently find it difficult to believe that discipline can coexist with creativity. Thus any discussion of creativity is expediently sidestepped, and for apparently good reason. Creativity thrives in freedom and, by their own brand of logic, any accent on creativity appears to run in the face of strong traditions and the military formalism that these institutions aim to strengthen and foster.

Our military and political leaders must become better informed about this resource, how to recognize it, and how to inculcate it in military leaders at every level and see that it becomes a useful weapon. As pointed out by Arnold Toynbee and other authorities, the suppression of this talent or the failure to use it as a national resource can be dangerous. Because creativity is earning a healthy respect among other professions and especially because it is proving useful to the Communists in formulating guerrilla strategy, it is urgent that U.S. military leadership take a careful look at this singular intellectual quality to determine those measures necessary to make a purposeful use of it in the management of military violence.

CHAPTER TWO

Military Genius Misinterpreted

No army can withstand the strength of an idea whose
time has come.

VICTOR HUGO

THE QUEST for the answer to how Napoleon won battles has
intrigued generals and statesmen since Austerlitz. Others
have sought to explain "The Nelson Touch," a special knack
at winning sea battles possessed by a handful of his navy's
admirals.

The truth is that a singular quality exists in every versatile
fighter, regardless of where he practices his profession. It
often spells on the battlefield the difference between
the brilliant innovator-leader and the plodding commander,
between the convention-laden infantryman and the light-
footed, quick-witted guerrilla. This quality in other professions is called creativity.

To a large extent convention and tradition are the main
enemies of creativity, and they are deeply rooted. Most
military maxims and modern military doctrines have evolved
from theories of participants in, and chroniclers of, battles

fought throughout recorded history. Maxims, particularly, have wielded a pervasive influence on current military thinking, even though some of them were formulated long before the crossbow or even the catapult. Although few of them will admit it, military leaders are unwary victims and willing purveyors of archaic and intellectually stultifying military dogma that kills the very initiative they praise so highly. Incredible as it may sound to the layman, serious, scholarly, military minds, ever seeking knowledge on how to win, bulge with clichés and conventional ideas that were uttered or written as long as 2,500 years ago and restated through the ages in a thousand forms in countless dialects.

The legendary Chinese general, Sun Tzu (circa 500 B.C.), is probably the first and most influential of these early voices. His *Art of War,* with its since overused title, distills his wisdom into an amazing number of catchy, often contradictory sayings, producing an umbrella of subterfuges to cover every ground performance on the battlefield. This oft-quoted treatise has excessively influenced the military minds of the world. Its formidable title is misleading because the book consists largely of rigid formulas or nebulous sayings, rather than discussion of the many aesthetic aspects of war. More than any other single work, it is guilty of channeling military minds into rigid beliefs, eventually leading to a practice of warfare that emphasizes bloodletting, guts, and massive slaughter. United States officers quote Sun Tzu to support infantry and tank warfare doctrine. Some theorists go so far as to use his maxims to explain the guerrilla's cleverness. As a matter of fact, Sun Tzu's maxims can be used to illustrate any type of battlefield maneuver executed since the beginning of warfare. Although the time may not be far off, no enterprising military writer has yet lofted him into space.

Although a number of other well-known works about

specific wars appeared in the interval, it was not until 2,000 years later that another substantial pseudo-military tract appeared. An Italian statesman and political philosopher, the crafty Niccolò de Bernardo Machiavelli (1469-1527), produced his own *Art of War* to add to his other equally famous works, *The Prince* and *Discourses*. He has become, undoubtedly, the most widely read and most influential writer on war and politics to appear in the Western World. Again, as with Sun Tzu, his attempt to convey the true meaning of art in war falls far short of the correct one, if he really gets to the point at all.

Three centuries later, Count (Marshal) Maurice de Saxe presented the military profession with his *Reveries on the Art of War*. Following de Saxe, several others produced works which have since become military gospel, including Frederick the Great (1712-1786), King of Prussia and founder of modern Germany, who, in his later years, produced the renowned military classic *Instructions to His Generals*.

From Napoleon, although he was not a writer of books, has come a number of "military maxims," which do scant justice to his incomparable military accomplishments. These accomplishments were codified by other authors, notably General Antoine Henri Jomini (1779-1869), at one time a staff officer to Napoleon, who later shifted his allegiance to the Czar of Russia and joined the struggle against his former chief. He remains probably the most venerated chronicler of battlefield methodology. Because of his staff experience, and because his book *Art of War* is an acknowledged source book of Napoleon's strategy, it has an authoritative ring and is widely quoted as justification for following prescribed formulas to achieve success in war. To have Napoleon, one of the finest military innovators of all time, presented as a proponent of rigid tactics only accentuates the difficulty in arguing the case for military creativity. Jomini thought in terms of rigid tactics—Napoleon did not.

It is of more than passing historical significance that Jomini's book went into a special printing in the United States just before the Civil War, and its wide distribution in both armies probably accounted in part for the fact that the war was largely a dull, brutal, unimaginative, slugging match. Jomini's maxims anesthetized many military intellects, especially because anything to do with Napoleon, master of the earth's greatest conflict prior to the United States Civil War, was held in such a high regard throughout the world, and his thoughts and deeds were gospel to all soldiers.

The domestically produced military textbook on tactics that was most widely read by members of both belligerent armies, and which was to have profound influence on the way the generals of both sides fought the war, was General William J. Hardee's *Rifle and Light Infantry Tactics*. Hardee had studied at the French Cavalry school during the 1840's and had been detailed to prepare standard manuals for infantry and cavalry tactics by the then Secretary of War, Jefferson Davis. Dr. Nathaniel C. Hughes, Jr., in his book *General William J. Hardee* wrote that Hardee's celebrated *Tactics* are, in truth, paraphrases from the French *Ordonnance du Roi,* an evolutionary form of Jomini's ideas, and fleshed out with additional—and usually superfluous—detailed instructions[1]. *Tactics*, with its emphasis on close-packed formations and complicated evolutions for deploying a column into line and for changing direction, was outmoded long before the war started. As a result, perusal of the Hardee manual actually did more harm than good to the neophyte officers of both armies who applied themselves so diligently to mastery of military evolutions. They could scarcely have been deliberately conceived more effectively to lead to the slaughter of thousands of riflemen in blue and butternut.

But the greatest of these is the early-nineteenth-century Prussian military and political thinker, Count Karl von Clausewitz. His treatise, *On War*, is an attempt at a comprehensive, philosophical study to determine how wars are won and lost. More wary than his predecessors, he tried to unfold the functioning of an intellect in battle crises but, except for some observations unsupported by any profound analyses or facts, quickly turned away from the vexing dilemma that he could not answer. He discussed, instead, some prosaic military matters and then wisely retreated into the sanctuary of political double talk, joining the company of Machiavelli.

Each of these oracles is revered and widely quoted to this day in the armed forces of all nations and, to a surprising degree, in contemporary America where the military mentality is supposedly strongly tempered by unique traditions of civilian control, an open warfare heritage, and a strong antimilitary philosophy.

American Army leaders have attempted to create a uniquely American philosophy of warfare from this mixed lineage of continental European tactics and native experience. But Clausewitz, Sun Tzu, Mahan, Jomini, and Lee have not properly crystallized United States military thinking. Instead, they have made it a hodge-podge.

Of the other American services, the Navy, probably because it started with little or no tradition or experience and fortunately came under the influence of the innovative John Paul Jones, is more creative than the Army. There are other reasons for this, which will be presented later. The

Air Force, meanwhile, once divorced from the Army and the stodgy Army mentality of the 1930's, has set the pace in the United States services with the degree of its military innovation.

The American situation is not entirely negative, however, because there is a flexible American countertradition of pragmatic techniques in combat, and a blending of the three mentalities that has been developed in spite of the older and more rigid European influences. Imaginative methods have been injected, frequently by the citizen soldier who has refused to permit his ingenuity to be smothered by orthodox military minds.

Why victory in war comes to some commanders easily, to some with difficulty, and to some never, in spite of the proliferation of written advice on the subject, frankly seems to remain an enigma. The ability to defeat an enemy in battle is still accepted as the only common denominator by which history's greatest military leaders are judged. These leaders, as well as their deeds, continue to be largely classified as accidents of history. Many of these leaders have won while leading paltry military forces and while faced with staggering physical obstacles and a strong, determined enemy. Although this is discussed in more detail in Chapter Five, it is merely introduced here.

Occasionally, success in war on land and sea is conveniently explained away in various written histories as a cunning application of "mass" or "maneuver" or "surprise" or some other of the "principles of war," or by one or more of the well-known maxims. Some startling victories, however, defy even the most imaginative attempts to explain them in classic terms. Often too, to the detriment of a proper understanding of warfare, a selected principle is warped to fit the circumstance. This purposeful distortion enables proponents of classic tactics and strategy to justify "immutable" tradition for the needs of limited intellects who are unable to see beyond or penetrate into the depth of the true intellectual character of great warriors and thereby understand better their operational resources.

Alexander the Great conquered the then known world with modest military forces and is, of course, a well-known example of a leader who, through an intangible gift, could be almost superhuman. He is one of the best known of the early military geniuses.

In 1206, human cyclones began to swirl down from the Mongolian steppes. They gained in fury, sweeping with tornado force into China, across the great plains of the Urals, then over the Ukraine to devastate the very heart of Europe. Genghis Khan and a succession of Mongol leaders, products of a nomadic society, headed these terrorizing forces. They did not fight wars in the later European sense of one professional army against another for limited objectives. They ruthlessly ravaged Turkistan and plundered the cities of Bukhara, Khiva, and fabled Samarkand. This human pestilence continued under Tamerlane who is said to have stacked a ghastly pyramid of 100,000 enemy skulls in front of the gates of captured Baghdad. Although each Khan proved a great conqueror, none had the benefit of formal military training. Operationally, they used no established principles of war, so far as is known, and whatever their military lore, in such distant areas, it had to be very flexibly adapted to the thousand contingencies they encountered as they engulfed country after country, defeating diverse and powerful forces. Although their lines of communication laced 4,000 miles through hostile countries, crossing deserts and the towering, snow-covered Himalayas, these intrepid warriors were never successfully defeated and, to the relief of Europe, voluntarily withdrew from the West when their greatest Khan died.

Hernando Cortez is another leader of comparable caliber. Landing near Veracruz in 1519, he set fire to his ships and with a paltry force of 250 men, 12 horses, and a few cannon and firearms turned westward and vigorously pushed into a seething hostile land. In less than a year he destroyed the Aztec empire, which counted its warriors in the hundreds of thousands. Such a brilliant conquest is not rare. Pizarro made a comparable conquest in Peru.

Few military leaders equal Francis Drake in accomplishments. On one occasion he set sail from England to America in two small ships, the larger, fifteen tons, hardly bigger than many a modern sailing yacht, and carrying a total force of seventy-three men. His intention was to storm Nombre de Dios in Panama, a town then as large as the port of Plymouth, England, for the purpose of capturing a hoard of Spanish gold. Nombre de Dios, described as the granary of the West Indies, harvested gold from Peru and Mexico and held it until convoys could be assembled to transport it to Spain. The sheer audacity of the venture still retains the power to astound. Drake operated thousands of miles from home, from a concealed base, and in the heart of a vast area governed by a hostile power. He had no official backing. Had he been defeated and apprehended, he and all his remaining force would have died on the scaffold as pirates or have been burned at the stake as heretics. Once he established his plan of attack, he carried the town in a matter of hours.

Three centuries later, a diminutive genius—his marshals and generals not the products of learned universities or military schools but instead the sons of poverty, revolution, and war—conquered Europe only to be brought up abruptly at the water's edge by England's Admiral Lord Nelson, an equally enigmatic character.

World War II brought some startling performers. German General Rommel, the Desert Fox, tied the British lion's tail in square knots during the North African campaign. On the other side of the world, Japanese Admiral Isoroku Yamamoto's use of bombers launched from aircraft carriers stunned the world at Pearl Harbor and introduced a whole new method of warfare.

In six days in 1967 Israel smashed a four-nation military alliance; severely damaged Soviet prestige in the Middle East; conquered an area four times her size; captured guns, tanks, missiles; and probably changed the entire politico-strategic structure in the Middle East.

Israeli equipment ranged from ultramodern to homemade. Taxicabs fought side by side with supersonic jets to blast enemy targets. They used ten tank models, from outdated to modern.

The military doctrine of the Israelis allowed subordinates great freedom of action and decision under broad directives, and encouraged initiative. The defeated opponents left little initiative for their division, and especially battalion, commanders.

"Surprise," military classicists claim, explains Yamamoto's success at Pearl Harbor. "Mass" or "maneuver," they will tell you, won the day for Napoleon at Austerlitz. A favorite principle is pulled out of the bag to suit each victory or, when the standard units of measure do not quickly or easily fit the circumstance, clichés such as "bold stroke of genius" or "brilliant intellect" are offered. Sometimes, indeed, when no principles or logic seem applicable, a shrug of the shoulders, a bewildered lifting of the hands with a *"C'est la guerre"* would suggest that no plausible explanation can be found.

Excessive adherence to "principles" and maxims or any form of fixed rule of war, I argue, is fallacious. Let us examine briefly one principle at random—"surprise." Surprise may occur, but it does so only at a given time or place and usually is a blend of many things, such as strength, the direction of the attack, and its proper timing. A battlefield surprise attack is also a tardy physical response hours, days, or even months after the leader had conceived the "surprise" operation. The idea had been, and always must be, conceived in the *mind* of a man before it is tested in battle.

For example, six months before he actually executed it so splendidly on the battlefield, Marshal de Saxe, unaided, formulated his 1745 Flanders campaign as it would and did unfold. Napoleon was noted for his forethought and habitually visualized his plans of action days and even months prior to their execution on the battlefield.

Bourrienne, his secretary, recounts how several weeks before the beginning of one of Napoleon's most decisive campaigns, he found the First Consul stretched on the floor with a large map before him.   ·

Pricked over the map, in what to Bourrienne was confusion, were a number of red and black pins. After a short silence the secretary, who was an old friend of school days, asked him what it all meant. The Consul laughed goodnaturedly, called him a fool, and said: "This set of pins represents the Austrians and this the French. On such a day I shall leave Paris. My troops will then be in such positions. On a certain day," naming it, "I shall be here," pointing, "and my troops will have moved there. At such a time I shall cross the mountains, a few days later my army will be here, the Austrians will have done thus and so; and at a certain date I will beat them here," placing a pin. Bourrienne said nothing, perhaps he may have thought the matter not "practical;" but a few weeks later, after the battle (Marengo, I think) had been fought, he was seated with the general in his military travel- ing carriage. The programme had been carried out, and he re- called the incident to Bonaparte's mind. The latter himself smiled at the singular accuracy of his predictions in the particular instance.[2]

Brigadier General Oscar Koch, General Patton's intelli- gence officer, illustrates this point—that the idea precedes the act.

One day in February 1944, shortly after my arrival in England, at what would later become Headquarters Third U.S. Army, I was summoned to General Patton's office. At the time, Patton had only a few staff officers and no assigned troops. He would, in March, take over the Headquarters of Third Army upon its arrival in England from Fort Sam Houston, Texas.

Upon entering the office I found General Patton leaning over a table alongside a wall, his back to me. I waited until he straight- ened up slightly. He asked me to join him. The index finger of his right hand remained in place on what was recognized by me as a Michelin Road Map of western Europe.

"Koch," he said, "I want all of your planning directed to here." His finger was pointing to Metz, and then with a wide sweep along the Loire River from west to east he continued, "I do not intend to cross the Loire, except to avoid a right-angled turn."

Chronologically, our conference took place at Knutsford, Eng- land, in February. His headquarters was to join him in late March. D-Day in Normandy would be June 6, with his Third Army to follow-up the First U.S. Army over the beaches of Normandy. The Third Army would cross the channel in early July and would become operational on August 1st, 1944. Patton's advance spearheading elements would reach Metz in early September, to be sat-down there, roughly seven months after designating Metz as his primary planning objective, from which, in spite of the campaigns of France, Avranches, Brest, to the Moselle, he never deviated.

What caused the selection of Metz, to me, is a matter of conjecture. Maybe his recollection of the days of the St. Mihiel salient of World War I; maybe the fact that it had never been taken since 451 A.D. by direct assault; maybe its siege in the war of 1870. Although its principal fortresses would have gone unchanged since the Franco-Prussian war, the terrain would be the same.[3]

This simple concept of the first importance of the mind has heretofore escaped most observers, despite the fact that it is the mind that produces victory, and all else becomes an adjunct to the idea it foments. I submit that the published ground and naval principles of war are limited tools that represent only part of the total effective arsenal of warfare.

Admiral Alfred Thayer Mahan, wary of principles of war and worrying about the dangerous overdependence that United States naval officers placed on such crutches, many years ago cautioned the profession, ". . . to no class of students is 'dogmatic prescription' more dangerous than to military and naval officers who, already disciplined, are prepared to accept rules, as rules without hesitation, and frequently with too little reflection."[4] Once embedded in naval instructions or army field regulations, he stressed, ". . . these so-called principles bind the minds of officers in unbreakable bonds."[5] Mahan's natural independence of thought prevented him from succumbing to the delusion, unintentionally and unfortunately fostered by such as Jomini, that war can be reduced to rules.

The true source of military power is too often wrongly considered to rest solely in the weapons of a nation—in its guns, missiles, ships, tanks, and airplanes. But this is a misrepresentation of history. Napoleon saw the truth and stated it well when he said to Comte Charles Tristan de Montholon at Saint Helena:

The . . . general is indispensable, he is the head, he is the all of an army. The Gauls were not conquered by Roman Legions, but by Caesar. It was not before the Carthaginian soldiers that Rome was made to tremble, but before Hannibal. It was not the French Army which reached to the Weser and the Inn, it was Turenne. Prussia was not defended for seven years against the three most formidable European powers by the Prussian soldiers, but instead by Frederick the Great.[6]

Yes, it was great generals who conquered, but what made them great was not their swords, their bravery, or their trappings, or their fearsome reputations. It was above all else the unique quality of their minds.

This quality lurks in the deep recesses of the subconscious mind. There, somehow, an idea is born. The idea is the product of experience, emotion, education, and the immediate environment. On the battlefield, the responsible leader must act alone. It is the leader's creative idea, more likely in the form of an intuition or a "flash of insight," which enables him to lead his men to the most significant victories. *These creative ideas do not spring from groups. They spring from individuals.*

CHAPTER THREE

Man, The Creator

I love power. But it is as an artist that I love it. I love
it as a musician loves his violin, to draw out of it
sounds and chords and harmonies. *I love it as an artist.*

NAPOLEON

MAN IS inherently creative. Although his creative ardor is
habitually dampened by external forces, his creativity, fortunately, bursts through in sufficient quantity to continue
his evolvement into something better than he was.

Galileo, the great innovator and inventor, astronomer and
physicist, born February 18, 1564, is considered by many
to be one of the greatest minds of all time. Nevertheless, he
aroused strong antagonism among the leading thinkers of
his day. His experiments leading to laws of bodies in motion
were in such flagrant contradiction to the teachings of
Aristotle, whose ideas had been the basis of scientific thought
in Europe for almost 2,000 years, that in spite of Galileo's
brilliant demonstrations, theologians and statesmen rejected
his concepts. His studies led him to the conclusion that the
sun rotates on its axis, and all his investigations confirmed
the Copernican theory of the solar system; but he did not
until 1630 dare to declare openly a doctrine too opposed to
accepted beliefs. Although it now seems incomprehensible,

at one time he was summoned to Rome where he was tried by the Inquisition and so harassed that he almost abjured all his beliefs. His tribulations are typical of many who have thought creatively and have brought new insights to mankind.

A growing, dynamic, and healthy civilization or an energetically productive organization is one in which there are a number of creative personalities with the courage to face the unfamiliar and to fight their own prejudices, as well as those of others, who are able to break through the inertia of the mass and inspire creative action. The character of this action will, in turn, hinge upon the ideas and actions of these individuals.

That an individual's success in the fine arts, science, and industry relies heavily on his creativity is now fairly well understood by participants in these fields because of a serious effort that has been made within them to learn about creativity and to apply it. Any standard discussion of these fields will normally concentrate very largely on describing something of the creative process from the inception of the idea to its adoption in a landscape, a symmetrical figure, or an invention. Prominent psychiatrists, psychoanalysts, philosophers, and artists elaborate on the creative process.

Unfortunately, this has never been the case in the works of any of the writers who have written on military affairs. This is particularly undesirable in view of the misleading impact of the common title or subtitle, *The Art of War*. It is deplorable that no serious military research is yet directed at unearthing the truth about creativity in a broad range of military affairs. Virtually nothing has been done in a practical sense to apply creativity to such concerns as personnel selection, strategic planning, research and development, and the winning of battles.

In eighteen articles I have examined on the subject of military leadership, published over the past four years in service journals, at best there was only casual reference to the intellectual function in the leadership task by seven of the authors, and four did not mention it at all. The remainder could be considered only by the greatest stretch of the reader's imagination to have referred to the use of the mind in combat.

One article (*Military Review*, September 1966) written by General Omar N. Bradley, whom I consider one of America's greatest battlefield leaders, a truly creative leader in the artistic sense, is particularly unenlightening. General Bradley asserts:

> The one who commands—military officer or captain of industry —must project power, an energizing power which coordinates and marshals the best efforts of his followers by supplying that ingredient for which they look to him, be it guidance, support, encouragement, or even *new ideas and imagination* [Author's italics].[1]

Except for a passing remark about new ideas this is all he has to say on intellect in leadership.

General Bradley falls into the traditional, cliché-ridden trap and resorts to discussion of physical energy, human understanding, and high ideals, discussed a thousand times and more in books and articles. General Bradley states, "The test of a leader lies in the reaction and response of his followers."[2] There is no mention of how the intellects of both leaders and led must be conditioned to get this response. But, despite this, the intellect is the key to achieving a coordinated and harmonious response between them, as I will explain later.

In the October 1966 *Military Review*, General Matthew B. Ridgway in an article on leadership supports the case for creativity in leadership, but he does not elaborate beyond an opening statement:

I incline strongly to the Wavell concept [that "no amount of learning will make a man a leader unless he has the natural qualities of one"]. While recognizing that there are many principles, or truths, pertaining to leadership, and while firmly believing that powers of leadership can be greatly increased in any individual through knowledge of these principles and practice in their application, I still think the variables of human nature combined with those of combat, and to a lesser degree with those in peacetime training, make the exercise of leadership far more of an art than a science.[3]

This is about the extent of what General Ridgway has to tell us about the function of art in leadership. What a wonderful opportunity the general had to leave his successors his word on how his ideas arose, and how he used them to manipulate men and machines of war to make the art he created in World War II and in Korea. But, unfortunately, the remainder of his article reverts to the thousand monotonies of physical fitness, self-discipline, physical courage, moral courage, and personal presence.

I would not quarrel with what these distinguished soldiers say if it had not already been said too frequently, to the complete neglect of the first and most important component of the nature of a leader—his creative intellect.

The fault, I suppose, is not theirs. They are, as I suggested above, the unsuspecting victims of tradition. But it is unfortunate, because what they merchandise is dangerous. They encourage boldness without brains, physical fitness before forethought, and presence before prescience.

Creativity studies are currently in vogue with industry and educators. These studies are making clear what painters, writers, and a few philosophers have known for a long time, that intellectual creativity is directly related to art. As new, unusual, creative ideas occur to an artist, he converts them into paintings. Someone brimming with high-quality ideas who has the energy and dedication of a true artist will produce many works of unique and superb quality. His works may become objects of reverence and awe to other men. These works come at the conclusion of a creative process of which intuitive or creative ideas are the igniting spark.

The business of how man can think up the very unusual things that have been breakthroughs, that have stemmed from the creative intellect, has perplexed man for many centuries. Man, the thinker, has sought man, the divine genius, who he is, how he thinks, and has feverishly hoped that fortuitous circumstances would arrange for him to reign supreme. This search was started by Plato with his concept of the philosopher-king, continued by Machiavelli, who proposed techniques for seizing and retaining military and political power, and furthered by Nietzsche's superman concept.

The search that faltered during the Dark Ages in Europe was later revived and is now pursued intelligently by American businessmen, scientists, and educators. It is no longer in the exclusive realm of philosophers and scholars because now it can be translated consciously into economic gain. During the days of *laissez-faire* capitalism, the Carnegies, Morgans, and Mellons created economic wealth through their individual efforts, but today corporation presidents are broadening the idea output by consciously tapping all of management's creativity to produce profits.

In order to understand the relationship of intellectual creativity to its military application and to perceive how this relationship can be used, it is necessary to understand some fundamentals.

Tolstoi, who struggled for years to define art and to determine its source, described the artistic processes in his book, *What Is Art?* It reveals conclusions that have helped to set a pattern for much of the thinking that has followed. He associates creation with art, and asks the question "What then is artistic (and scientific) creation?" His answer is:

... it is such mental activity that brings dimly perceived feelings (or thoughts) to such a degree of clearness that these feelings or thoughts are transmitted to other people[4]... A really artistic production cannot be made to order, for a true work of art is a revelation.[5]

As another author explains:

A new idea often comes to the discoverer like a flash of lightning, apparently unwarranted, often in the most inappropriate circumstances. At that moment he may not even be in a position to prove the soundness of his idea; theoretically, he simply knows it is true; he senses it.[6]

The creative idea may be deeply buried in the subconscious, making itself difficult to identify. Creation begins typically with a hazy, even a confused, excitement—a sort of yearning or hunch. Frequently, the creative worker is quite unready consciously for the novel development about to issue from his mind. Pasteur frequently had valuable intuitions that skipped far ahead of scientific proof, reached later with logical but laborious, scientific processes. The idea may come all at once and without preliminaries; sometimes it may be very incomplete—a mere suggestion serving only as a clue, to which substance must be added by much additional and diligent work—occasionally it may be almost complete in character. Although there are varying beliefs concerning the mechanism of the creative process, there is general agreement that rapidity and spontaneity are its primary characteristics.

David Ogilvy, a leading advertising executive, stresses:

. . . the creative process requires more than reason. Most original thinking isn't even verbal. It requires a groping experimentation with ideas, governed by *intuitive hunches* and inspired by the unconscious. The majority of businessmen aren't capable of original thinking, because they are unable to escape from the tyranny of reason. Their imaginations are blocked.[7]

Relating his personal involvement in this magical process, he says:

I am almost incapable of logical thought, but I have developed techniques for keeping open the telephone line to my unconscious, in case that this orderly repository has anything to tell me. I hear a great deal of music. I am on friendly terms with John Barleycorn. I take long, hot baths. I garden, I go into retreats amongst the Amish. And I take frequent vacations, so that my brain can lie fallow—no golf, no cocktail parties, no tennis, no bridge, no concentration; only a bicycle.

While thus employed in doing nothing, I receive a constant stream of telegrams from my unconscious, and these become the raw material for my advertisements. But more is required; hard work, an open mind and an ungovernable curiosity.[8]

Businessmen, long dragging their heels, finally harkened to the benefits suggested by the Ogilvy approach, and now tend to rely more and more on freewheeling creative individualists. Corporations are coming to de-emphasize committees and to stress individual responsibility. A significant number of companies are becoming disenchanted with conformity-minded organization men and, instead, are placing new stress on individuality, originality, and unorthodox approaches in their executives. While such men usually upset

management, it has discreetly contended with the tribulations involved because of the increased production and sales
realized through the greater use of innovators.

The trend in many forward-thinking companies is away
from the sort of man typically sought in the past—the middle-
level executive whose major aim in life is to do his company's
bidding. Unfortunately, not all management has comprehended the essential features of creative thinking, for instance, that all types of people are potentially creative when
they are working with intense motivation and self-discipline
and the right environment—the last an important feature
for nurturing a high degree of creativity.

Everything that is known about the creative process indicates, curiously enough, that the *conscious* state of mind has
little or nothing to do with the original conception of what
one writes or composes. Mozart, for example, wrote most of
his gayest melodies while suffering agonizing physical an-
guish and mental pain. Balzac dashed off his *Droll Stories*
while rebuffed in romance, pursued by creditors, laughed at
by society, and wrapped in the gloom of loneliness. Robert
Louis Stevenson was wracked with the pain of terminal
tuberculosis when he was turning out his charming adventure tales. Edgar Allan Poe conceived some of his finest
poems and classic mystery stories, *Murders in the Rue
Morgue, The Gold Bug*, and many others, when plagued by
physical misery, by poverty, and despair. There are thousands of such cases in the history of all the arts.

Freedom, which is a very personal feeling and related
closely to how one feels in one's surroundings—one's daily
association with people, organizations, laws, religion, and
clubs—appears to be an important ingredient to the kind of
environment that will stimulate creativity. Einstein once
said, "The development of science and of the creative activi-

ties of the spirit in general require what is another kind of freedom characterized as inward freedom."[9] The creation that comes from scientists proceeds from the free operation of their minds. Most important advances in science or in any field will continue to be unexplained, unpredictable, and even unpalatable to others, and it is essential that the men who are to make such advances should not be prevented from doing so by the obstructionism of others.

Frequently, and unfortunately, a society that limits freedom or frowns on its expression, refers to the consciously free practitioner as "unconforming." His lack of conformity, which society finds so unpalatable, is frequently only a creative or artistic individual's rejection of the mode of society as he attempts to throw off that mode to the extent that will allow him to go about his creative work.

Very young children teach us some remarkable things about creativity. They enter life free from the restrictions, the modes, and patterns of society; they fail to conform and remain free as long as their innocent minds are not unduly hampered by social mores transmitted to them by adults. Initially, children are spontaneous and intuitive but are soon curbed by their elders who, themselves conforming to society's will, start making the children do what society expects of "good" children. In any case, the child is more apt to show creativity than the adult who, due to the buffeting experience of life, goes along to get along.

Studies show that creative people are inclined to be extremely flexible and able to adjust to intellectual change, but sometimes less so to physical environment because everyday practical considerations bore them. They have all kinds of responses to a single idea. They are skillful with the tools of their trade, whether dealing with sound, color, symbols, or objects. Usually they have an intense interest in the world, especially in its more puzzling aspects. They try to observe it accurately and bring order from disorder.

The military services are particularly critical and repressive of the innovative types. The Italian Giulio Douhet, the apostle of total warfare, did a tour in prison for his heretical ideas. General "Billy" Mitchell was tried, found guilty, and forced to resign from the Army—condemned on the charge of "making statements to the prejudice of good discipline." But fellow aviators know that the real reason for his trial and conviction was that his ideas differed from those accepted as doctrine by the War Department. Another well-known rebel and nonconformist was General Claire Chennault. Although he had trouble getting along with his military contemporaries because of his far-reaching ideas and soon found himself retired, nevertheless, many of his rejected ideas proved quiet usable in the Far East during World War II, where he commanded the Flying Tigers.

General George Kenney, formerly of the United States Air Force, points out:

His [Chennault's] fighter tactics are accepted even today as models. With a handful of aircraft constantly starved for fuel, bombs, spare parts, and replacements, and opposed and hampered by the antiquated thinking of his army superiors, Chennault's achievements are without parallel in the story of air power in World War II. In no other theater was so much destruction caused to the enemy by so small a force.[10]

Much effort is required to nourish and prepare the mind and activate it. It is necessary to acquire and master new knowledge, gather facts, observe, explore, experiment, and develop technique and skill—all the conscious activities that prepare the mind for its creative role. The labor required to do all this is extensive and arduous enough to repel many from participation. The most energetic mind, the most cre-

ative one, must attain mastery of the field in which he is to
act and be strongly motivated toward getting done what
needs to be done. Thus, activity requires skill in the appropriate means of expression; that is, an artist may have the
greatest of creative ideas, but unless he is able to use his
paintbrushes adeptly, unless he can mix the paint to exact
tints, and unless he has some knowledge of the elements of
perspective, his ideas will never materialize into the con-
figuration his mind sees. Beautiful ideas unsupported by
tutored skill *rarely* have the power to open the future.

Somerset Maugham says it this way:

For the production of a work of art is not the result of a miracle.
It requires preparation. The soil, be it ever so rich, must be fed.
By taking thought, by deliberate effort, the artist must enlarge,
deepen, and diversify his personality. Then the soil must lie
fallow. Like the bride of Christ, the artist waits for the illumination that shall bring forth a new spirit life. He goes about his
ordinary avocations with patience; the subconscious does its
mysterious business; and then, suddenly springing, you might
think from nowhere, the idea is produced.[11]

Admiral Mahan expresses a similar viewpoint when com-
menting on Admiral Nelson, hero of the battle of Trafalgar.
In this battle, Nelson proved fully equal to the challenge of
the professional task because he possessed genius in war.
As Mahan remarks, Nelson's intellectual faculties, though
not unsuspected, had not been allowed scope for their full
exercise, his victories at the Nile and Copenhagen notwithstanding. His fleet was larger than ever, his authority un-
challenged. Mahan continues:

Before him [Nelson] was now open a field of possibilities
hitherto unexampled in naval warfare; and for the appreciation of
them was needed just those perceptions, intuitive in origin, yet

resting firmly on well-ordered, rational processes, which on the intellectual side distinguished him above all other British seamen.[12]

He had already, in casual comment about the military conditions surrounding the former Mediterranean campaigns, given indication of that perception, which, Mahan adds:

... is the indispensable complement of intellectual grasp and insight in a moral power, which enables a man to trust the inner light, to have faith, a power which dominates hesitation, and sustains action, in the most tremendous emergencies, and which, for the formidable character of the difficulties it is called to confront, is in no men so conspicuously prominent as in those who are entitled to rank among the great captains.[13]

CHAPTER FOUR

Creativity,
Your Unexpected Ally

The result of a battle hangs on a thread and is mostly
the outcome of a sudden thought. One approaches the
enemy according to a prearranged plan, one comes to
blows, one fights for a while, the critical moment draws
near, a spark of inspiration flames up—and a small reserve division does the rest!

NAPOLEON

THE LONG HISTORY of the arts has led to some understanding
of the creative processes that culminate in the artistic masterpiece. In military ranks, however, by comparison, there is,
as I have said, no similar development of comprehension of
the artistry of creative combat. Largely responsible for this
is the practice of excessive adherence to rigid military tradition, often at the expense of innovation. At fault is the host
of narrow-minded academicians who have written on the
art of war without understanding the creative source of art
itself.

Before it is possible for the military man to understand
the nature of creativity, he must understand some of the
fundamentals about it in relation to art—fundamentals which,

in fact, apply to all creative pursuits. Intellectual creativity that gives man majestic works of art is a vital, moving process. A knowledge of the intellectual sources and processes that lead to the intuitional, the exciting, creative idea is as necessary to the professional soldier as it is to men in other fields of endeavor.

Either because of timidity, or lack of foresight, or possibly through lack of knowledge, the military historian, the military analyst, and the military man himself have not used the information the philosophers have presented on intellectual creativity. This information, coupled with the more recent discoveries and viewpoints on the subject of creativity expressed by students of human behavior, should be compared with the performance of leaders in war to determine if there are any useful relationships. In addition to the Chinese Communists, as already briefly pointed out, the Russians seem to be aware of this. The Soviet Defense Minister, Marshal Malinovsky, recently emphasized:

... a large role is played by the creative mind of the general, commanders, and initiative of personnel in armed combat, alongside theoretical military knowledge. ... Creativity in armed combat constitutes human activity based on objective laws. In the process of this activity more perfected forms of combat equipment and new forms of troop organization are created, as well as more favorable combat conditions, new means and methods of conducting combat operations.

The activity of commanders of all ranks includes elements of creation. The making of a decision for combat, and the fulfillment of any mission presuppose a certain measure of an innovator approach to the matter, for there are no absolutely identical combat situations. Each decision has its own specific and non-repeated conditions of the battle or operation. The highest degree of creation is innovation, when man lays basically new roads in military science and in the art of warfare.[1]

The responsibility for failure to weld together art and military leadership must be partly borne by the military itself. The idea that the military leader is an artist is not quite palatable to hard-bitten professional soldiers, and there are four reasons why this is so:

Art is considered to be the opposite of science. That war is a science rather than an art is a widely held belief of the military profession.

Art is beautiful and creative. War is grim and destructive. Because of this contrast, man is confronted with a thought-provoking question: How can a military leader be a creator, when one of his objectives is not creation but destruction?

Art implies the aesthetic. It is associated with immortal works of music or with great paintings. Professional military men seldom associate art with the blare of bugles and the roll of drums, with a cavalry charge, with ominous mottled gray ships bristling with guns and missiles, or with silver-sleek jets.

Creativity is dangerous to discipline. There is a fear in the military mind that to permit creativity is to allow anarchy, which is utterly incompatible with the idea of a smooth-functioning, hard-hitting military force. This fear, like most fears, is nourished by ignorance and is completely unwarranted. There can be freedom under laws—this is the philosophy of our form of government, and under it this nation has flourished.

An understanding of the nature of creativity explains why one individual becomes a brilliant leader while another, who is as well educated and from the same professional environment, does not. Moreover, a study of the creative element to be found in the thought processes of the leader offers a plausible explanation for victories attained throughout the history of warfare.

To understand why a creative military leader is fundamentally an artist, it is first necessary to understand what creativity and art actually are.

One prominent school on the subject suggests two types of creativity, identified here as type "A" and type "B."

Type "A": Deductive Creativity. Edmund W. Sinnott refers to this type of creativity as primarily deductive, a creativeness developed by "direct frontal assault."

It consists in marshalling the widest possible array of facts or ideas and then carefully searching for heretofore unrecognized relationships between them. This seems to be the method used by Edison, for example, in his inventions, and by Einstein in the development of his theoretical ideas.[2]

In the military experience, the commander's estimate of the situation, for example, is an attempt to channel creativity of this type into a productive pattern, to ensure inclusion of all elements of the situation, thus forcing the birth of a logical decision. It is a safe, ponderous method frequently applicable where time is not of the essence. Military staffs use deductive creativity to plan operations. In all fairness, it must be said that, particularly during the twentieth century, type "A" creativity has won drudging battles and wars. The mass-slaughter frontal attacks on the World War I Western Front and Operation Overlord, the World War II cross-Channel plan for the invasion of France, demonstrated this fact. This is a workable but costly method for correlating the vast resources of tremendous political-industrial complexes to the waging of war.

Type "B": Dynamic Creativity. With this type, which bears close resemblance to intuition in the way it works, it is much more common for a new idea to rise almost spontaneously in the mind, often seemingly out of nothing. It may have the character or feel of a hunch, and it is often referred to as "intuitive" thinking and is most commonly associated with the best of artistic achievement. Eliot D. Hutchinson, describing this type in his book *How to Think Creatively*, tells of an incident related by the noted English historian, Edward Gibbon:

> One day in Rome, Gibbon, according to his autobiography, sat musing on the ruins of the Capitol. Robed, barefoot friars were singing vespers in the Temple of Jupiter. Suddenly, *like a burst of light*, the inspiration for a monumental work, *The Decline and Fall of the Roman Empire*, came to him—its outline vague, its content as yet unforeseen. But there it was, a central, expansive idea, a keynote or motif that was to grow and gather accretions of material to itself until it was finished seven years later [Author's italics].[3]

We are told of a "sixth" or intuitive sense possessed by Field Marshal Rommel. It saved him many times from personal injury in combat and served as the basis for his victories. While he watched a tank battle in North Africa, he suggested to his aide they move to another hill. They moved to the hill some hundred yards distant and almost at once a thunderous shelling was rained on the site they had just left. On another occasion, Rommel told one of his staff officers that he intended to evacuate his headquarters within an hour because he felt "in his bones" that it was about to be raided. They moved. On that night British Commandos raided the headquarters to find it vacant.

It is evident that General Douglas MacArthur had a similar gift. As with many great soldiers, his creative strategy was the product of his own intellect and conceived at unusual moments. Clark Lee and Richard Henschel in the book *Douglas MacArthur* relate how MacArthur decided to take the greatest gamble of his career—the history-making and decisive Inchon landing in Korea:

He began planning for an amphibious landing at Inchon, far to the north of the battlelines, which, if successful, would decisively change the course of the war. He made his decisions while flying over Korea—in noting that the rice crop was ready to harvest. He had been considering an amphibious operation, and now he determined to "get that crop and not let the North Koreans have it."[4]

A similar story is related about Admiral Low, an American naval officer who served as Operations Officer to Admiral Ernest King, Commander in Chief of the United States Naval Forces in World War II. Low, an idea man, came up with one that invigorated a whole nation whose morale was sagging sadly after the Pearl Harbor tragedy. His restless mind searched for some positive success that would restore American confidence. He found it while in Norfolk inspecting the construction of the aircraft carrier, USS *Hornet*. As he was taking off on the return flight to Washington, he glanced out of the plane window and saw below, marked off on the ground, a practice airstrip about the size of a carrier's deck. The idea he so desperately needed struck him. He presented to Admiral King the next day a proposal that longer-range Army aircraft take off from a carrier to bomb Japan. The world remembers the outcome—the Doolittle raid on the heart of Japan, limited perhaps in military value, but of inestimable worth in raising American morale.

In a paper prepared for the Chief Historian, Headquarters, European Command, Generaloberst Dr. Lothar Rendulic stated, from his experience as a division commander fighting on the Russian front:

A decision, therefore, is not a *problem of simple arithmetic,* but a *creative act*. Even in instances in which a decision is not the outcome of lengthy deliberations, the way leading to a decision involves a complicated mental process in which, among other factors, also the *temperament* of the individual finds expression. *Intuition and a keen sense of perception* play a considerable role. Even if the commander has a large quantity of reference material at his disposal, and even if he has sufficient time for careful evaluation of all known factors, it still remains true that *the process by which a decision is reached is, in the final analysis, nearly always a secret which, in most instances, remains insoluble even to the person who has arrived at the decision* [Author's italics].[5]

Viscount Montgomery of Alamein holds that:

... a C.-in-C. of great armies in the field must have an inner conviction which, though founded closely on reason, transcends reason. It is this which will enable him at a certain moment in the battle—the right moment—to take a short cut which will take him to his objective more swiftly and more surely than equally careful but less inspired commanders.[6]

Similarly, ideas often manifest themselves in original scientific research. Dozens of scientists have testified that their best ideas came to them when they were sleeping, or fishing, or strolling, not while they were consciously grappling with the problem.

We have scarcely begun to recognize the enormous power of the unconscious mind, which is the true source of creativity. Newton, the great mathematician, lying under the apple tree, discovered more truth than Newton browsing through books and poring over papers.

Dynamic creativity is a common phenomenon. Harold H. Anderson stated with respect to this type:

It is found among all sorts of men and women who have been faced with the need, sometimes a consuming, passionate desire to gain a new insight into truth and beauty, to solve a problem in science, to bring to life a painting out of pigment, oil, and canvas, or to set a poem down in words.[7]

Schopenhauer, the German philosopher, took the view that art, which generally comes from the "intuitive" creativity, is greater than science:

... the latter proceeds by laborious accumulation and cautious reasoning, while the former reaches its goal at once by intuition and presentation; science can get along with talent, but art requires genius.[8]

William James, one of the few American philosophers to achieve recognition in European intellectual circles, contended that truth can never be discovered by logical reasoning alone. He felt that truth is essentially irrational. He believed that there are many basic facts that transcend logic, which are seemingly irrational or unreasonable and yet fundamentally true. "We must," he said, "learn to give up logic, fairly, squarely, and irrevocably" as a philosophical method: for "reality, life, experience, concreteness, immediacy, use what word you will, exceeds our logic, overflows and surrounds it."[9] Doctors M. B. Parloff and J. H. Handlon, eminent psychologists with the National Institutes of Health, further claim that "creativity may in fact require the temporary suspension of logic in order to permit freer play of fantasy and imagination."[10] Many recent scholars of human behavior agree concerning the importance of nonrational thinking.

The central point of the *élan vital* philosophy of Henri Bergson places strong emphasis on intuition as opposed to intellect or reason. Bergson's feeling is that man must transcend the intellect if he wants to get a real and direct glimpse of reality as it is. He would support the *deductive* creativity classified under Type "A," but he contends that man must also use something akin to instinct — namely, direct insight or intuition — to correct the distorted picture of reality which the intellect presents to us. He feels that the normal absorption of impressions by the intellect is a useful and valuable picture of the world about us, but it is still only a picture, a very incomplete and imperfect one. We must use, for instance, the data of science, but it must correct the world of reality by the use of intuition in order to construct a complete picture. It is only through intuition that man is able to seize reality itself. In Bergson's estimation, intuition, not logic, is the basis not only of philosophy but of all forms of artistic endeavor. "The clearest evidence of intuition is in the works of great artists." He asks, "What is it we call genius in great painters and poets and musicians? It is the power they have of seeing more than we see and of enabling us by their expressions to penetrate further into reality."[11]

William M. McGovern, in his work *From Luther to Hitler*, says that what is true of the artist is also true of the leaders of society and the state. The heroes of human history are those who have had a greater direct insight into reality than their fellows.

Dr. Frank Barron at the University of California's Institute of Personality Assessment, who has done promising research on creative people, comes to several significant conclusions:

Creative people are especially observant, and they value accurate observation . . . more than other people do.

They often express part-truths, but this they do vividly; the part they express is the generally unrecognized; by displacement of accent and apparent disproportion in statement they seek to point to the usually unobserved.

They see things as others do, but also as others do not. . . .

They are born with greater brain capacity; they have more ability to hold many ideas at once, and to compare more ideas with one another—hence to make a richer synthesis.

... they are by constitution more vigorous and have available to them an exceptional fund of psychic and physical energy.

Their universe is thus more complex, and in addition they usually lead more complex lives. ...

They have more contact than most people do with the life of the unconscious—with fantasy, reverie, the world of imagination.[12]

While man would tend through rationalism or deduction to minimize the emotional or passionate decisions, nevertheless, he is, fundamentally, an emotional and passionate creature. While man's belief should wisely agree with reason, there are many situations which occur that reason alone cannot solve. Consequently, man adopts the irrational approach to a problem, and usually this approach is motivated by passion and emotion. As the abrasion of combat wears through the thin veneer of civilization, it grinds off structured thinking and man's passions gain ascendance. His intellect is freed to perform creatively, relying on intuition, and he can have a field day of unfettered expression during the maelstrom of conflict.

Karl von Clausewitz, concerned about the intangibles of how to win in combat, made a futile effort to penetrate the fog of war. Although as a military and political theorist he made some worthy contributions, his writings show only a limited conception of intuition's role in war. For example, he gropes warily:

This very peculiar difficulty must be overcome by a mental gift of a peculiar kind called *sense of locality*. ... It is the capacity for quickly forming for oneself a correct geometrical representation of any given piece of country and consequently of correctly and easily finding at any time one's position in it. This is obviously an act of imagination. The perception, no doubt, is formed partly by the physical eye, partly by the intellect, which by means of judgments derived from knowledge and experience supplies what is wanting, and out of the fragment visible to the physical eye forms a whole.[13]

Clausewitz adds:

War is the province of uncertainty; three-fourths of the things on which action in war is based lie hidden in the fog of a greater or less uncertainty. Here then, first of all, a fine and penetrating intellect is called for to feel out the truth with instinctive judgment. . . .

Now if it is to get safely through this continued conflict with the unexpected, two qualities are indispensable: in the first place, an intellect which even in the midst of this intensified obscurity is not without some traces of inner light which lead to the truth and, next, the courage to follow this faint light. The first quality is figuratively denoted by the French expression, *coup d'oeil* [quick glance], the second is *resolution*.[14]

Clausewitz continues his dissertation with a strong ring of authority on the concept of intuition; he then later describes *coup d'oeil* as "more frequently, the mental eye that is meant. It amounts simply to the rapid hitting upon a truth which to the eye of the ordinary mind is either not visible at all or only becomes so after long examination and reflection."[15]

Later Clausewitz comments:

All thinking is indeed art. Where the logician draws a line, where the premises, which are the results of cognition, stop and judgment begins, there art begins. But more than this: even cognition by the mind is again a judgment and consequently art, and, finally, so too is cognition by the senses. In a word, if it is as impossible to imagine a human being possessing merely the faculty of cognition without judgment as it is to imagine the reverse, art and knowledge can never be completely separated from each other. The more these subtle elements of light embody themselves in the outward forms of the world, the more widely separated their realms become; and now, once more: where creation and production is the object, there is the domain of art; where investigations and knowledge is the goal, there science reigns. After all this, it is obvious that it is more fitting to speak of art of war than "science of war."[16]

To the extent that Clausewitz realizes the difference between a long examination and reflection and a rapid perception of the truth, he visualizes correctly the separation between *deductive* and *dynamic* creativity. In the papers discovered after his death was an unfinished manuscript that included possibly his best thought with regard to instinctive judgments in war:

The theory of war on a great scale, or what is called strategy, presents extraordinary difficulties. It may perhaps be said that on its different subjects very few people have clear ideas—ideas, that is to say, which are logically traced back to their underlying necessity. In action most men follow a mere *instinctive judgment*, which hits the mark more or less successfully, according as they have in them more or less of genius.[17]

Curiously enough, General George C. Marshall's philosophy that leaders of troops should be required to make up their minds quickly with scant information expresses a similar viewpoint. He sought, therefore, to teach the art of innovation to extricate tactical principles from the procedural formulas in which they had become fixed by the school men.

The eminent American naval historian and authority on naval strategy, Rear Admiral Mahan, author of *The Influence of Sea Power Upon History, 1660 to 1783,* and *Naval Strategy,* is one of the few prominent military theorists to visualize and identify the relationship creativity has to war:

. . . Art, out of materials which it finds about it, creates new forms of endless variety. It . . . partakes of the freedom in the human mind in which it has its roots. Art acknowledges principles and even rules; but these are not so much fetters, or bars, which compel its movement aright, as guides which warn when it is going wrong. In this living sense, the conduct of war is an art, having its spring in the human mind of man, dealing with various circumstances, admitting certain principles, but beyond that, manifold in its manifestation, according to the genius of the artist and the temper of materials in which he is dealing.[18]

To Thomas Edward Lawrence searchers for the meaning of art in war owe a particular debt of gratitude. This mystical "Lawrence of Arabia," whose stature as a leader of unconventional forces and innovator in warfare is not wholly recognized, most clearly identifies the role of art and intuition in war. For good or evil, what he has discovered can, in my opinion, be one of the greatest contributions to the future of mankind. It is buried in a few pages of his *Seven Pillars of Wisdom*. Even the discerning reader finds it difficult to discover, no less than to comprehend. If military men have found the essence of the meaning of intuition in war in this work, then the evidence is that, except for the Chinese Communists, they have failed to profit from it.

Lawrence, that baffling, thoroughly unmilitary genius, grasped the essence of creativity and insight in war purely by his own intuition. Bedridden, wracked by sickness and despair after the campaign to take Hejaz, he pondered the direction his war should take to break the Turkish shackles. Lacking the men and guns of his opponents, his task seemed insurmountable. To a lesser man it would have been.

Weighing the teachings of Clausewitz, de Saxe, Jomini, and Foch for answers to questions on his war, Lawrence ultimately rejected them, saying they:

... disgusted me with soldiers, wearied me of officious glory, making me critical of all their light. In my case, my interest had been abstract, concerned with the theory and philosophy of warfare especially from the metaphysical side.[19]

Thinking of a Turkish shortage of supplies and a dependence on railroads, Lawrence mused:

The death of a Turkish bridge or rail [line] . . . was more profitable to us than the death of a Turk. In the Arab Army at the moment we were chary both of materials and men. Governments saw men only in mass; but our men, being irregulars, were not formations but individuals.[20]

In pursuit of the ideal conditions we might kill Turks because we disliked them very much, but the killing was pure luxury. If they would go quietly the war would end. If not, we would urge them, or try to drive them out. In the last resort we should be compelled to the desperate course of blood and the maxims of a "murder war."[21]

Thus did Lawrence begin to formulate a far-reaching philosophy that was to guide his conduct of the war and end in Arab victory.

Suppose, he thought:

. . . we [Arabians] . . . were an influence, an idea, a thing intangible, invulnerable, without front or back, drifting about like a gas? [Traditional] armies were like plants, immobile, firm rooted, nourished through long stems to the head. We might be vapour, blowing where we listed. *Our kingdom lay in each man's mind;* and as we wanted nothing material to live on, so we might offer nothing material to the killing. It seemed a regular soldier might be helpless without a target, owning only what he sat on, and subjugating only what, by order, he could poke his rifle at [Author's italics].[22]

Separating the individual soldier from the mass to function as a free agent apart from the structure of formations, "intangible," a force free to maneuver where it chose, the intellect free and supreme, Lawrence transferred to guerrilla warfare some of the fundamental conditions and the rationale for creativity as we understand it now. In so doing he turned intellect to the task of making up for the difference in force. Other far-reaching effects of Lawrence's philosophy will be covered in Chapter Ten.

CHAPTER FIVE

Creative Leaders Mystify Analysts

> It is hardly possible to discuss the spirit of any army apart from that of its commander. If in strategy wholly, and tactics in great part, success emanates from a single brain.
>
> COLONEL HENDERSON

CREATIVE LEADERS simply do not fit easy patterns, although ordered minds often expect them to. Previous attempts to find why certain military leaders decisively win battles and wars have proved largely ineffective over the years. We are heirs to a profusion of often conflicting and confusing conclusions, although it must candidly be admitted that specific successes can often be precisely explained. Obviously, much can be attributed to superior intelligence, broad education, professional training, and courage. However, no single one of these can be found in equal quantity in each commander, and in some are largely lacking.

Consequently, a simple way out of an embarrassing dilemma is to use the subterfuge of calling an accomplished

46

military leader a "genius." The term "genius" as thus applied does not sufficiently define that which we are seeking. If the terms means, or is specifically modified to include, "creative genius," then "genius" might be appropriate.

Today, because we understand better the mechanism of genius, much success in warfare can be perceived as attributable to creatively talented intellects performing a historic role as artists in combat. It is this creativity which has boosted men to genius, the genius which many have so blithely described. Creativity, the long-unrecognized essential ingredient to military competence, cries out to be revealed to man in its true relationship to warfare.

However, to find well expressed statements by qualified military practitioners in victory presents some difficulties. It is indeed a rare occasion where they will have recorded for posterity or revealed to their enemies something of the creative intellectual processes that led them to select successful action on the battlefield. Few great captains of history have had the sense of history or the necessary time and patience to tell about it in detail in the same manner as have men in more leisurely fields of creative endeavor. Rather we are now forced to observe their actions and achievements in historical context, to, in fact, establish a case from circumstantial evidence that their achievements stemmed from creative ideas or from an environment conducive to creative expression. However, a sufficient body of such circumstantial evidence does exist.

Alexander is probably the first notable, highly creative, military leader about whose personality and conquests there exists fairly detailed information. His personality showed many creative characteristics. For example, Plutarch tells us he supplied the inspiration for his armies while his able generals performed the more mundane tasks:

[The generals] contributed organization, training, tactics, and strategy. He led his troops by the brilliance of his imagination, the fire of his unstudied oratory, the readiness and sincerity with which he shared their hardships and griefs.[1]

When younger, he was free to follow his own inclinations. Leonidas trained the boy's body, Lysimachus taught him letters, Aristotle tried to form his mind. King Philip of Macedon, Alexander's father, was anxious that Alexander should study philosophy "so that," as he said, "you may not do a great many things of the sort I am sorry to have done."[2] Alexander was an ardent student who was too soon consumed with responsibilities to reap the full rewards of formal instruction. Like so many men of action, he wondered that he could not be also a thinker. Plutarch said:

He had the violent thirst and passion for learning, which increased as time went on. He was a lover of all kinds of reading and knowledge, and it was his delight after a day of marching or fighting to sit up half the night conversing with scholars and scientists.[3]

However, as Will Durant states in *The Life of Greece*, "Royalty found him at twenty, after which warfare and administration absorbed him; in consequence, he remained uneducated to the end."[4]—a consequence not necessarily a disadvantage to the creative type.

Alexander inherited the freedom won by his father, the conqueror of Greece. At Corinth, Philip had convened a federation of Greek states, of which he had been unanimously chosen chief. Each state pledged him men and arms and promised that no Greek anywhere would fight against him. Philip was assassinated by one of his officers in the year 336 B.C. Alexander, who promptly seized the throne, inherited a unified nation and a loyal strong army that idolized him. With this army Alexander overcame all local opposition and prepared to conquer the world. He faced no laws except those imposed by his own will and heeded few social customs. There were few kings of comparable stature against whom to compare his conduct or actions except Darius of Persia. Few commanders in history were treated so kindly by circumstance — few has destiny prepared so admirably to harvest circumstance so well.

Stories of Alexander's conquests are legion, but a few will be mentioned here to illustrate how his rich intellect, now unleashed and completely unrestricted, got results. He prepared for the invasion of Asia. Soon he crossed the Hellespont without opposition, having what seemed to the haughty rulers of Asia a negligible force of 30,000 footmen and 3,000 cavalry. A Persian army of 400,000 troops tried to stop him at the Granicus. The Greeks lost 115 men, the Persians 20,000. He then marched south and east, taking cities and receiving surrenders for a year. Meanwhile, his formidable opponent, Darius III, gathered a horde of 600,000 soldiers and adventurers; it was such a force that six days were required to march them over a bridge of boats across the Euphrates River; he had no less than 600 mules and 300 camels to carry the royal purse alone. When the two armies met at Issus, Alexander had no more than 30,000 followers from various Greek city states, but Darius stupidly chose a field in which only a small part of his multitude could fight at one time. When the slaughter was over the Macedonians under Alexander had lost 450 men, the Persians 110,000, most of them being slain in wild retreat. It is said that Alexander forded a stream on the corpses of his enemies.

In 331 B.C., he succeeded for a second time in defeating Darius, whose combined forces had swelled to 1,000,000 men. Alexander, hardly stopping in his eastward movement, marched over the mountains in the dead of winter to seize Persepolis. Leading his armies, he moved far and wide over the expanses of the Middle and Far East, conquering wherever he went, subduing all those who put forces in his way. In 327 B.C., he crossed the Himalayas into India, there to staggeringly defeat the armies of the Indians.

Summing up the evidence supporting Alexander's creative talents, we find brilliance, imagination, an immersion in warfare and the ways of war, a growing fund of all kinds of knowledge and experience, an impatience with formal learning, a freedom of activity accorded him throughout his lifetime. There were few, if any, laws to which he had had to adhere for, after all, he, and his father before him, were the law, and although in Greece he was the arbiter of custom and undoubtedly influenced by customs, he escaped them in Asia. Here he was absolutely free in both the intellectual and the physical sense. He had virtually attained a breakthrough, resulting in the ideal environment for optimum mental and physical freedom of action. His subsequent conquests are legend — his achievements unparalleled. Only death finally stilled the creative artist in Alexander.

Approaching Alexander in creative stature was the wily Hannibal. "It is said that the Romans could not readily forgive him for winning battles with his brains rather than with the lives of men. His tricks, his skill at espionage, his subtle strategy, his clever tactics were beyond their appreciation. . . ."[5] Hannibal operated quite free of restraint from his native Carthage. As a matter of fact, the Carthaginian politicians, safely at home in North Africa with the Mediterranean separating them from the Roman legions, seemed to abandon the Roman problem to their great general, hopeful that he had a military solution.

After Hannibal completed his perilous midwinter crossing of the Alps, it is estimated that he had remaining for his campaigns in Italy between 26,000 and 30,000 men. Yet, he faced monumental odds. Rome is said to have raised a force against him totaling 300,000 foot soldiers, 40,000 horsemen, and 456,000 reserves.

One army, under the first of several famous Scipios, met Hannibal along the Ticino, a small river flowing into the Po at Pavia. Hannibal's Numidian cavalry put the Romans to flight.

At Lake Trasimene, Hannibal encountered another Roman army, 30,000 strong, led by the Tribune Caius Flaminius. With part of his forces, Hannibal decoyed this army into a plain surrounded by hills and woods that concealed most of his troops; at his signal the hidden columns debouched, fell upon the Romans from every side, and killed nearly all of them.

In 216 B.C. he drew the Romans into the classic battle of Cannae, where, through the stratagem of "double envelopment," fighting at the head of 19,000 battle-hardened troops, 16,000 unreliable Gauls, and 10,000 horsemen, he placed his least reliable troops — the Gauls — at the center of his forces, probably expecting that they would give way. They obliged, and when the Romans followed into the pocket they left, the subtle Hannibal, himself in the thick of the fray, ordered his veteran fighters to close in upon the Roman flanks and, in conjunction with this move, ordered his cavalry to smash through the opposing horsemen to attack the Roman legions from behind.[6] Surrounded, the Roman army floundered, lost all means of maneuvering, and was virtually annihilated. Of the 86,000 Romans who went into the fray, 44,000 fell, including one of their generals, Paulus, and 800 senators who had enlisted as soldiers. Hannibal had lost 6,000 men, two-thirds of whom were Gauls. It was a supreme example of generalship, never surpassed in history. As an authority says, "It ended the days of Roman reliance upon infantry and set the lines of military tactics for 2,000 years."[7]

Hannibal was forced to improvise means as he went along — from the doctoring of his horses to the sale of his prisoners of war. He was constantly finding unexpected ways out of his difficulties. He invented, as it were, a course of action that no one could predict. Sempronius, Flaminius, Marcellus, and a long roster of Romans tried to outguess him, and guessed wrong. Hannibal had a way of changing his plan almost in mid-stride. While moving up the coast of Spain in 218, he shifted overnight to the incredible plan of the march through the Alps to Rome. Then, instead of marching to Rome after Cannae, he changed his strategy to the formation of the Mediterranean alliance and the economic squeeze of the enemy capital. At Zama he came into the field with a formation entirely unexpected by the astute Scipio. From first to last his actions filled the Romans with astonishment. No one else ever managed to hide an entire army above a mist through which the enemy marched unsuspecting or to transform an open plain like Cannae into a death trap.

No one else except Alexander managed to maintain an army on a hostile continent for nearly a generation. Again, as in the case of Alexander, the free environment Hannibal enjoyed undoubtedly played an important role in allowing his intellect to realize its full creative potential.

Hannibal was away from his home base from 218 to 201 B.C. His accomplishments can be considered no less than phenomenal when compared with the obstacles he had to overcome — the modest army he commanded, the lack of cooperation from his own Carthaginian government, the fact that he operated entirely on foreign soil and amid formidable geographical obstacles frequently surrounded by hostile nations.

Julius Caesar was a middle-aged politician and an amateur at war when he began his military career. He had received the usual basic training of every wellborn Roman. However, not until he took his command in Gaul in 58 B.C., at age forty-three, did he begin the climb that would fit him into the small circle of universal leaders — Alexander, Hannibal, Napoleon.

Caesar was no theorist about war. He was the complete man of action, possessing a rare ability to make the correct decisions on the spur of the moment. In his great battles, at Alesia in Gaul, Pharsala in Greece, Thapsus in Africa, and Munda in Spain, he showed an uncanny ability to read the enemy's mind and strike the enemy's weakest point. In battle he was a magician in armor, a leader whose flashing eyes and scarlet cloak seemed everywhere at once, instilling his soldiers with the certainty of victory.

Except for our first two wars, an overwhelming abundance of economic power has been the deciding factor that has given the United States arms its victories. America has been inclined to rely on raw strength to the neglect of brains. Hannibal gives us a warning that we, as a nation, should heed. It is that ". . . warfare need not be a vast conflict of technological skills and accumulation of weapons of destruction. Regardless of its mechanisms, war remains a matter of human beings, directed by their minds. It has never ceased to be an art, in which a supreme artist may appear out of a pass of the Alps to prevail over money- and man- and weapon-power. No amount of stockpiling of things can completely offset superiority of minds. In 219 B.C., the Roman state was prepared for war in the usual manner; the Carthaginian was not. Of all that befell both the Romans and the Carthaginians the cause was one mind — Hannibal's."[8]

A contemporary Russian antagonist of Napoleon, Field Marshal Aleksandr Suvorov, who was never directly beaten and who lived by the principle of intuition, rapidity, and impact, drove the French from upper Italy in 1799. John Paul Jones several times visited the field marshal's headquarters, understood him from the start, and ranked Suvorov with such soldiers as Alexander, Hannibal, Caesar, Gustavus Adolphus, Marlborough, and Frederick the Great. He thought that the Russian ranked with the first in all Europe alive at the time.

General Archibald Wavell says:

Suvorov proved a leader quite above the ordinary rules of military criticism. His energy was as inexhaustible as it was audacious. He taught his followers to trample, as he did himself, on every difficulty in their way. Obstacles only provoked him to strike out new resources; and wild and irregular as he was, he possessed in a remarkable degree that intuitive sagacity in the hour of battle which is one of the highest qualities of military genius.[9]

Dying in 1800 at the age of seventy-one, he left the field to his equally intuitive contemporary, Napoleon.

Napoleon and his biographers provide us with some of the earliest and most convincing written evidence of the play of intuition and the creative intellect in war. Creativity of the intuitional variety best explains Napoleon's sweeping successes as well as his ultimate defeat. Napoleon shattered the ring around France and marched on the crest of the flood tide of revolutionary thought and action released by the French Revolution. In his *Great Captains, Napoleon,*

Theodore A. Dodge, an eminent military historian, tells us:

Napoleon's mental equipment was in all respects noteworthy, and showed itself in many ways.... His power of intellectual application was *unlimited and his mind singularly elastic;* ... His *intuitions* were so clear that logical processes seemed unnecessary to enable him to reach a true conclusion; and the speed, certainty and comprehensiveness of his mental work were likewise remarkable. Details never blurred his appreciation of the whole and he always aimed at great results [Author's italics].[10]

How many of Napoleon's characteristics — as a general or even earlier as a cadet in the year 1785 — compare with some of the traits of creative people! A certificate received from his military school states:

Reserved and laborious, he is more fond of study than any pleasure; likes to read good authors; very *diligent in abstract sciences,* little enquiry in others, he knows thoroughly mathematics and geography, *silent, loves solitude, obstinate, haughty,* exceptionally given to egoism, *talks little,* is energetic in his actions, *prompt in action* and *severe in meeting opposition;* has much self-esteem, is ambitious in striving for all things. This young man is worthy of being favored [Author's italics].[11]

Napoleon executed a timely arrival in history. The Revolution, with its conscription, had begun to cut itself loose from the old manner of conducting war, but no one great leader had arrived to put his seal upon the emerging method and to fashion it into a permanent form. There had been men of talent, but not a man of the very first rank; and no one quite broke away from the past. Then came Napoleon with his genius and power to create; he threw the old behind him; in his march from Nice to Leoben, for example, he laid the foundation of the new system of war. In his operations in that eventful year he exhibited every phase of his new creation. Thus, for instance, the leaders of the Revolution did in effect discard the magazine system of Frederick, but they had not learned to live on the country to the extent Napoleon taught them to do. They left the old, but they did not create the new. This was reserved for Napoleon — he not only made war nourish war, but he showed men the value of masses and of interior lines, how to put the most men at the key point of fighting, how to divine the key point of the field and to throw overwhelming numbers upon it. Bourrienne quotes Napoleon as saying, "The art in war consists in always having with a smaller army more forces than the enemy at the point where you attack, or where you are attacked."[12]

While this principle of war of thrusting massive blocks of grenadiers at the critical point of the enemy's lines was one of his most important creative contributions to warfare, he also made many other innovations. Napoleon always felt that he could categorize war, that he could place it into narrow channels, that he could itemize his actions, and to a great extent he did this in his maxims. In the final analysis, however, he realized that waging war was something of the intuitive, something of the indefinable.

Napoleon's maxims are riddled with contradictions. It may be that it was a simple stratagem of the Napoleonic intellect to confuse his opponents with a multitude of highly contradictory maxims or principles which, because of their number and diversity, they could never hope to analyze; thus they remained uninformed as to his creative talents. The highly contradictory nature of Napoleon's actions versus his stated beliefs is no better expressed than in Dodge, who says:

In the opening of his remarkable campaign from Nice to Leoben, Bonaparte in his operations enunciated and approved the value of the mass theory. In the operation from Mincio east-

ward, he had apparently put aside the mass theory, and had divid-
ed his forces. This has led to the expression of opinion by some
historians that Bonaparte did not believe in or act on his own
maxims, that every campaign must open up a new theory of
action, and that after all nothing can ever be done by rule. This
is only in the narrow sense true. Napoleon wrote to the King of
Spain in September, 1808, "The art of war is an art which has
principles which it is never permitted to break." At St. Helena
he truly said, "All great captains of antiquity, and those who
later more worthily trod in their footsteps, have only accomplished
great results by adhering closely to the rules and to the natural
principles of the art;" and, "the principles of the art of war are
those which led the great captains whose deeds history tells us
of."[13]

Dodge then concludes with this pointed observation: "As
a matter of fact no one adhered more fully to this theory
of war than Napoleon; but he knew when to make these
exceptions and when to gauge his operations by the character of his opponent."[14]

Napoleon inwardly understood better than any of his
opponents the need to deviate from accepted principles.
He realized there was something more than just logic in
winning battles. For example, in his maxims, possibly one
written later in his career when he had a better opportunity
to reflect upon the nature of war, he states:

War is composed of nothing but surprises. While a general
should adhere to general principles, he should never lose the
opportunity to profit by these surprises. It is the essence of genius.
In war there is only one favorable moment. Genius seizes it.[15]

In what is undoubtedly one of the most penetrating
maxims Napoleon ever stated, there are some very enlighten-
ing observations that bear very strongly upon his realization

of the importance of the creative or intuitive idea in its relationship to the battlefield:

The qualities to command an Army are born in one. — A general never knows anything with certainty, never sees his enemy clearly, never knows positively where he is. When armies are face to face, the least accident in the ground, the smallest wood, may conceal part of the enemy's army. The most experienced eye cannot be sure whether it sees the whole of the enemy's army or only three-fourths. *It is by the mind's eye, by the integration of all reasoning, by a kind of inspiration, that the general sees, knows and judges* [Author's italics].[16]

Napoleon finally gets to the point when he says:

The general never knows the field of battle where he is to operate. His vision and *insight* come from *inspiration;* he has no positive information; the data for arriving at a knowledge of localities are so fortuitous that *almost nothing is learned by experience.* It is a faculty to be able, first to grasp instantaneously the relation of the ground with the general nature of the country. It is finally a gift *called a military eye, which great generals have received from nature* [Author's italics].[17]

Independence, the ability to go it alone — these and other similar formidable traits of the creative intellect — Napoleon possessed. In his early campaigns, while yet a lackey of the Revolutionary Committee in Paris to whom he had owed his advancement, he nevertheless refused to subordinate himself. He conducted these early campaigns without consulting anyone, insistent in the face of the guillotine-wielding Paris government that he alone was the master of his actions. His plans were so idiosyncratic, as typical of "oddball" intellect, that leaders of the several armies to whom he occasionally suggested them sent them back with little patience. General Kellermann wrote back, referring to one of the plans, "... The originator [Napoleon] belonged to an insane asylum . . ."[18] and General Schérer suggested to Paris that "the man who made the plans for the army of Italy had better come and carry it out himself."[19] It is no tribute to Kellermann and Schérer that they fell into the timeless trap, typical of those who do not understand the creative intellect, of failing to realize the novelty of the creative idea that someone produced who was able to see more clearly in the environment in which they lived, but that they, because of their inflexibility, did not perceive.

This rejection by intransigent authority has almost been a rule throughout history in fields of artistic endeavor. Creative men constantly find themselves ahead of their times. Napoleon was more fortunate than most warriors in having favorable circumstances in which to practice his craft. In the case of some painters, for example, their art was not appreciated until some time after their death. The painting "An Arrangement in Grey and Black," more commonly referred to as "Whistler's Mother," painted by James McNeill Whistler, for many years was not accepted by the best galleries. However, his "new" idea finally overpowered the inflexible ones of his imperious critics, and it is exciting to note that the work, which at one time was unacceptable, was insured for $500,000[20] when finally brought to America in 1932. In final vindication of Whistler, the painting now hangs in the Louvre. Its value? — priceless! Modigliani, the Impressionist, died a pauper. In his lifetime, few of his paintings sold, yet he is today considered one of the great painters of the world. The public was blind and intolerant to both these artists. They not only differed from the conventions of their contemporaries in their art, but were superior to many of them.

Napoleon in war stood as other artists have stood in other ages, in other areas of man's endeavor. Ideas tumbling pell-

mell from his creative mind exploded onto the battlefield.
It took fifteen years for his opponents to shrug traditions,
stodgy thinking, and outmoded patterns of war to understand Napoleon's art and then to move abreast of this art.
In those fifteen years, Napoleon had exhausted his creative
talent to conceive his finest art and then went into a steep
decline. His energy was dissipated, but only after his
creative talent had built within Europe a new system of
political, legal, and military order of which significant ves-
tiges still remain. He succumbed, less the victim of superior
coalition forces than of a circumscribing social, political,
and military strategy and tactics, brainchildren his opponents
now recognized. Napoleon was no longer able to create
anything new.

The proud French army performed heroically at Waterloo.
However, the contest was not determined in lives, or in
territories gained or lost. These materials were only mutilated, external evidence of a yet formidable military mind
deserted by its creative spirit.

Turning to the Western Hemisphere, undoubtedly two
of the most brilliant and creative leaders produced in Latin
America are Simon Bolívar and José de San Martín. These
two towering military leaders threw off the yoke of Spain
throughout South America in military campaigns that from
many standpoints compare with the best of Hannibal and
Alexander. Their armies, small in manpower, performed
superhuman feats — crossing the treacherous Andes, struggling through tangled rain forest under primeval conditions
to beat decisively, time and time again, the well-drilled
regiments sent by the Spanish Alcaldes to stop them. Each
performed superbly as an independent personality, quite
alone and above the commands of any government, functioning without impediment as his creative intellect dictated,

and with no national boundary to restrict him. Their campaigns have been grossly neglected by students of military history.

Taking a look at another campaign, more familiar to North Americans, we find that during the Civil War General Lee entrusted operational freedom to only two of his officers — General "Stonewall" Jackson and cavalryman General J.E.B. ("Jeb") Stuart. Both of these officers functioned best in an environment of minimum supervision. In the Valley Campaign, Jackson, it is recalled, completely on his own, outwitted and defeated consistently superior Union forces. In a similar vein, General Stuart's raid of October, 1862, into Pennsylvania was a brilliant creative masterpiece shunning accepted methods. There were no conventional tactics involved, no observable conformity to traditional principles of war. It was sheer inspirational, creative, artistic genius at work. General Lee also showed the virtue of creativity. He had the confidence of his President and was virtually free to make his own military decisions. He functioned independently and, at times, at long distances from Southern borders.

A statement by hard-slugging General Grant seems best to portray not only his own unimaginative philosophy but that of the Union generals as well. At a brilliant innovative peak during the Vicksburg campaign, he about-faced when given command of the Union armies. He became a butcher, surpassing, in his lack of creative ingenuity thereafter, all of his lackluster predecessors. When once asked about the art of war, Grant replied: "The art of war is simple enough, find out where your enemy is, get at him as soon as you can, strike him and hit him as hard as you can, and as often as you can and keep moving on."[21] Fortunately for Grant, he had enough men and guns to feed into the jaws of war, so that this type of mentality could be supported. The United States has further been fortunate in having enough manpower and massive industrial resources in the wars since to be able to perpetuate this way of thinking on a grand scale. The same opinions among some of our generals during World War II have made critics claim that we drowned the Germans in equipment rather than by clever strategy.

The illiterate, but able Confederate General Nathan Bedford Forrest, fortunately unable to read Jomini or Hardee, ungoverned by any polished military background, seriously upset conventional Northern generals and undoubtedly a lot of stuffy Southern superiors. John Allen Wyeth in tribute to Forrest says:

> . . . even in moments of extreme peril, so rapid was the process by which his brain registered and analyzed every detail of the picture which flashed through it, that any action which the emergency demanded followed as logically and as quickly as the roar of the thunder follows the lightning flash.[22]

The ordinary mind can deal with reasonable certainty and success with the things that are expected, but to cope successfully with the unexpected is a crucial test of extraordinary ability. In war, and especially upon the battlefield, it is the unexpected which most often happens, and in these great emergencies the mind is too often dazed by the rapid and kaleidoscopic changes which are occurring, or temporarily stunned by the shock of an unlooked-for stroke. As in nature everything that grows holds its perfection but a single moment, so in the crisis of human affairs a single moment of time holds the key to success or failure.

Mercurial General George S. Patton of World War II is an outstanding example of the creative military intellect. He is best remembered for his resolute independence and for doing things differently. He was quick to seize an opportunity and exploit it to its fullest; he rode over opposition, and he was rarely fettered by convention. Whether it came about by purpose or sheer accident, his assignment at the open south flank in France suited his battle artistry. It gave him freedom to create as he wished, and, what is important, plenty of open country so that he could and did vent his creative energies without geographic limitations.

General Rommel surpassed Patton as a creative intellect. It was Hitler himself, early impressed by Rommel's unorthodox military ideas, who quickly perceived his potential to a militarily awakened new Reich. When Hitler's Italian allies, sorely pressed by Commonwealth forces, began to waver, he placed Rommel at the head of the crack Afrika Korps. Here Rommel's genius and military philosophy in operations on the battleground became painfully evident to his enemies.

Rommel shunned military formalism. He made no fixed plans beyond those intended for the initial clash; thereafter, he tailored his tactics to meet specific situations as they arose. He was a lightning-fast decision-maker, physically maintaining a pace that matched his active mentality. In a forbidding sea of sand, he operated in a free environment. Once Rommel ruptured the British lines in Africa, he had the whole northern part of the continent opened to him. Comparatively free from the hamstringing authority of Berlin, disregarding orders even from Hitler himself on occasion, and now in a free intellectual and physical environment, Rommel implemented one successful operation after another until he had most of North Africa under his control and Cairo trembling at his feet. Hitler, determining to reinforce the Russian front, diminished the normal flow of supplies and reinforcements to Rommel, preventing him from exploiting his advantage. In an ideal creative environment, he created military art at its best. In sharp contrast, Field Marshal Rommel in Normandy, under the gaze and close control of Hitler and Von Rundstedt, could not perform in his Afrika Korps spirit.

In an interesting twist of history, General Montgomery took over command of the British forces in Africa and turned the tables on Rommel. Montgomery again exhibited much the same type of creativeness when he, in turn, broke out from the German positions at El Alamein and stitched Rommel's lines to the seacoast. Still, Montgomery in North Africa was not the same as Montgomery in northern France, where he, too, had to operate under the dour gaze of the Supreme Commander, the supervision of a dull Headquarters, and the eagle eye of his Prime Minister.

While Rommel, Patton, and Montgomery fought creative battles in the narrow confines of the European land mass, a new type of war began to develop in the Pacific, opened by the attack upon Pearl Harbor. Never before in the history of warfare had there been such an area — a vast ocean with tiny islands widely separated one from another. Two nations were locked in the titanic struggle, each of vastly different political philosophies, each with modern weapons virtually untried — such as aircraft-carrier fleets, umbrellas of flak thrown above vast surfaces, navies, land-based air fleets, and Kamikaze squadrons. The novel circumstances requiring enormous coordinated complex operations involving amphibious landing, air cover, and naval bombardment gave an exciting creative turn to war. Consequently, from this environment grew some of the outstanding leaders of World War II on both sides and some of the finest evidence of battle innovations, such as the surprise attack at Pearl Harbor. This performance took daring and courage, but above all it also took an enormous creative talent on the part of the Japanese.

Japanese creativity reached a high-water mark at the capture of Singapore, the bastion of the British Empire in the Far East. Realizing the sea approach to be impregnable, the Japanese chose to attack the city through the uncharted Malayan jungles from the direction where the British fortress was most vulnerable.

Some six months later American creativity assumed ascendancy, halting Japanese southward expansion by the use of massive air-to-sea attacks on their fleet. Thus, the Pacific became the spawning ground for countless innovations in the art of warfare.

General MacArthur, after his first bitter battles against the Japanese in New Guinea, took a long hard look at the scene unfolding in the vast Pacific arena in light of his now exhausted troops and short supply of weapons and equipment. Replacements trickled in to give him only the minimum strength he needed to conduct pressing operations. To push back the Japanese by direct attacks against the maze of enemy-held islands would prove costly and a long effort. He was confronted by the terrifying facts of geography — the magnitude of the Southwest Pacific Theater proved almost an unsurmountable task of conquest and control. His lines of communications from the United States to the scene of operations were some of the longest in the world, harassed by the as yet undefeated Japanese Navy.

MacArthur had some unusual ideas for solving the problems facing him. As General Charles Willoughby and John Chamberlain quote General MacArthur in their book *MacArthur, 1941-1951*: "My strategic concept for the Pacific Theater contemplates massive strokes against only main objectives, utilizing surprise and air-ground striking powers

supported and assisted by the fleet."[23] He felt that new
conditions such as he now encountered required new and
imaginative methods. "Wars," he said, "are never won in
the past."[24]

MacArthur's new type of warfare had no precedent in
history. Here was the type of warfare this intuitive and
insightful mind gloried in. It took creativity to formulate
and fight it, courage to implement it, plenty of valor to
slug it out, and heroes to die for toeholds on the bleak coral
beaches of key islands in the virtually impregnable Japanese-held areas.

Seemingly, then, the only things these brilliant innovators
had in common were keen intuition and an environment
sufficiently free from the fetters of tradition to permit them
to use it fully.

CHAPTER SIX

Intuition — Essence of "The Nelson Touch"

The quality that distinguishes a great captain is that faculty of quick and instant action in which all the processes of thought and will blend into one over-powering conviction and *impulse that lesser men never know* [Author's italics].

MAHAN

IN CONTRAST to the ground commander who during peacetime must serve on land masses under the sway of social, political, and military controls of his country, the commanding officer of a naval vessel or task force is more fortunate. During peace and war, the creative art is a constant companion of the officer commanding at sea. Once he shoves off from shore, he is alone on a frontierless waste of sea that imposes few restrictions to his movements. He is often in a constant mortal contest with a hurricane or a high sea whose actions can be less predictable than those of a human enemy. The naval officer must make frequent decisions to contend with the elements successfully, and in so doing he hones sharp the razor of his intellect. Unhindered by ponderous staffs, free from the political and social fetters that often bind the ground commander, he is ready to apply his own adaptations of the hard-learned lessons of peacetime to the art of war. His ideas are needed quickly and frequently, and he must be prepared to select the useful ones as they come to him to solve particular problems.

The course of history has been thwarted, turned, or strengthened more quickly and more conclusively at sea than it has on land. The sea provides frequent occasions for the exercise of creativity. For this there are several reasons. In naval battles the commander in chief of large forces is either personally visible, or the ship on which he sails is visible to others of the fleet through normal vision or by electronic means. Because of this he has greater and more personal control over the situation. He can dominate his forces more directly than can a commander on land, whose field of view is limited, whose range of operations is restricted by tactical boundaries, and whose speed over land is frequently two and one half miles per hour, the marching speed of the foot soldier.

Perhaps the two most important factors in a sea battle may be said to be timing and weather. As Commander R. F. Seymour, a member of Admiral David Beatty's staff during World War I, states: "An attack made a moment too soon may be a stroke in the air and an attack made a moment too late a missed opportunity which will probably not occur again in many months."[1] It is the successful sea captain observing the whole pattern of events who is able to sense the appropriate time to launch an intuitively derived action.

Also important is the intense professionalism in the Navy, a factor vital to creativity. For its skipper, commanding a ship is a twenty-four-hours-a-day, seven-days-a-week job for as long as he is at sea. He manages his ship and crew, is constantly responsible, pressed to be alert, and frequently required to render decisions. This builds a useful fund of experience that is available to his intuitive faculty when critically needed.

Communication between the naval commander and his crew is more easily attained than it is by military leaders in other services. A ship is, to a great extent, a complete, self-sufficient community.

The image of the total personality of the captain in the minds of the crew is a vivid one. They know how he thinks and they know his peculiarities. It is relatively simple for a captain to visit virtually any part of his ship and, particularly on smaller ships, there is frequent and personal contact with each crew member. He has quick voice communication with the critical control centers of the ship, and he can obtain rapid and ready response to his commands. Operation at sea and constant communication between captain and crew develop a oneness of personality.

The naval officer at sea is also freer because on many of the vessels he is permitted complete operational latitude once he has his orders. A destroyer commander may be given wide latitude in the mission he is to perform. A captain of a submarine may have a completely free hand in a particular area. Thus, they are fortunate to have the freedom on which creativity thrives.

On the other hand, the finest infantry officer is far more restricted by the nature of the situation under which he has to operate. He has limited contact with his troops once they are committed, great distances to travel to visit units, unreliable communications, restricted visibility, sketchy information of the enemy, political considerations, and unforeseen land obstacles. Working with such bits and pieces, it takes an enormous amount of brilliant and coordinated effort to be a successful infantry commander. The missions of an Air Force pilot may be quite intermittently scheduled. A mission may keep him operating his airplane and commanding its crew in air space for from one hour on a fighter attack to many hours in a strategic bombing raid. This contrasts sharply with the task of a submarine captain, who may be on his mission for several months. The possibilities for innovative action are, then, less frequently presented to the Army or Air Force officer than to his naval counterpart.

Perhaps the best Navy command to study in detail for evidence of innovative possibilities is the submarine. The expression of, or the existence of, many of the elements of creativity so far discussed are easy to detect since a submarine represents a capsule environment about which there is an extensive quantity of source material available. The achievements of American and German submarines in two wars have been phenomenal when one is realistic about the handicaps each submarine captain has faced. Submarine service draws something extra and mysterious from a man that makes him excel; this something extra is a high degree of creativity, because all elements are ideal for its expression. Otherwise, the submarine could not, just as a technological device alone, perform as it does, nor could its presence be so feared, its achievements so formidable.

Confronted with many disadvantages, frequently traveling alone in a vast and hostile sea, out of communication with friendly forces, unable for long periods of time to surface and see the light of day or the stars of night, relentlessly hunted, the submarine captain, with unbelievably small resources, has proven frighteningly effective in two wars.

Like other military writers, naval historians have long groped for that magic ingredient that makes a brilliant captain. Until Admiral Mahan appeared, it had not been effectively synopsized, and since Admiral Nelson, for a lack of description or a better definition, the naval profession of the world has referred to it as "The Nelson Touch." Napoleon and other monarchs have constantly sought naval leaders with similar virtuosity to command national sea power, but the failures to find them have been more notable than the successes. While Napoleon despaired of his admirals, Great Britain cheered for hers.

The accounts of some early naval actions such as those fought by Themistocles at Salamis and Formio in later Greek and Persian wars show highly creative men at the helm of winning naval forces. However, as is frequently the case, historical records are incomplete or mythical, and cannot be considered to be scholarly sources. Consequently, we must pass on to naval actions where historical records give us an accurate report of the personalities involved.

It was not really until the discovery of the Americas by Columbus and the subsequent colonial ventures of the Western European nations that we begin to find an accumulation of reliable information. Expansions brought power struggles between greedy European nations intent on gold and verdant land. Imperialism was no longer directed toward expansion on the Continent, but toward newly discovered lands thousands of miles away, a circumstance that forced various nations to strengthen fleets in order to have sufficient sea power to protect their growing commerce with overseas possessions. Although the major contest lay between England and Spain at first, decided by the defeat of the Spanish Armada, there were also some lesser conflicts which produced brilliant captains such as the Dutchman

Michiel de Ruyter. It remained for Trafalgar to give Nelson his niche as a respected naval commander and public figure whose actions and accomplishments were public knowledge. His naval achievements were diligently recorded, and from these records the true nature of his leadership can be studied. It is quite evident from the majority of Mahan's writings that, in his opinion, Nelson is a prime example of the original thinker of the intuitive type, a true military genius.

Several forerunners of Nelson helped shape the spirit of naval thought by their frank and daring departures from tradition. Edward, Lord Hawke, one of these great captains, defeated the French fleet in Quiberon Bay in 1759, thereby checkmating a potential French invasion of England. Mahan recounts Hawke's Quiberon Bay decision.

Hawke was a total stranger to the waters of the bay, but they were completely familiar to his antagonist. In hot pursuit of the French fleet, with one of his ships already in contact with part of the enemy's rear, with several ships of his fleet ahead of him, and his own position situated just south of Belle Isle, Hawke took a bold action. The French admiral, in familiar waters, was leading his fleet over rocky shallows to force the pursuing British fleet either into an untenable position or to shy clear of the rocks and thus break contact.

Hawke took the lead position in order to signal his fleet the directions to take from moment to moment because the course was so perilous. Ahead of Hawke, at the southern extreme of the shoals which acted as a breakwater for Quiberon Bay, were formidable rocks known as the Cardinals. The French admiral passed around these successfully soon after the firing began between the rear of his fleet and the forward elements of the British. Hawke approached, but he did not have an experienced pilot to lead him through the treacherous waters.

The unenviable duty as pilot for the British fleet in this case fell on the shoulders of the sailing master of Hawke's flagship. However, this hapless man, in completely strange waters, possessed no knowledge of the area before him and, unfortunately, was not able to rely on his imperfect charts. While the risks ahead were known by all, it was that master's duty to caution Hawke of the difficulties.

The operation, however, was one vital to England's cause. Informed by his sailing master of the risks ahead, Hawke replied: "Now lay us alongside the French Commander-in-Chief."[2] To show the intuitive nature of Hawke, Mahan relates:

At dusk, the British fleet, under the unswerving impulse of its leader, moved steadfastly forward to meet a combination of perils that embraced almost all that a naval captain could be called upon to face—darkness and intricate navigation, a lee port fringed with outlying and imperfectly known reefs and shoals, towards which all were hurried by a fast rising wind and sea that forbade all hopes of retracing their steps during the long hours of the night. But Hawke pressed on. The obstacles overcome, he won a resounding battle following his decision to forge ahead, a decision fraught with dangers that was rendered of the moment.[3]

Considerably earlier, in 1588, when the very existence of England was threatened by the Spanish Armada, it was saved by a clever departure in naval warfare. Whether it was the intellectual child of Sir Francis Drake, Vice Admiral of the fleet, or his superior, the tactic adopted by the English to close with the majestic Spanish galleons of the Armada, near enough to get the smaller English craft under the lowest tier of galleon guns, won the historic battle for them. Here, they could stay beneath the trajectory of Spanish fire while their broadsides shattered the lower decks of the Spanish galleons. The Spanish admiral later frankly admitted he could not cope with this novel tactic.

Many historians believe America's struggle for independence was greatly enhanced by the French victory over the British fleet outside Chesapeake Bay. If this is the case, America's future was also assured by a creative act of French Admiral François de Grasse. Admiral de Grasse flaunted tradition that, theoretically, would have called either for a mass debouchment from the bay, or the forming of a line for a sally from the bay that would have permitted the British ships to pick off the leaders of the line one by one. Instead, de Grasse chose to infiltrate his ships by small groups out of the area and into the sea, there to reform. The British admiral, waiting for the line to sail forth, failed to realize what was happening until it was too late. By that time, most of the French fleet, having issued forth and formed a formidable line of its own, could proceed to defeat the British.

The ensuing defeat of the Redcoats by the Continental Army under George Washington at Yorktown was fundamentally a result of the inability of the British fleet, shunted away from the Chesapeake by the clever Frenchman, to support its troops on land.

Admiral Nelson's conduct of sea battles presented a series of innovations, starting with an original battle plan and proceeding through quickly conceived alterations to its successful conclusion. He stamped his personality on each victory. Another characteristic was that once he announced his main battle plan, he gave wide latitude to his lieutenants to use their own ingenuity and initiative.

In the Battle of the Nile in 1798, Nelson mutilated the

French fleet and gave the British uncontested command of the Mediterranean, thus isolating the French forces under Bonaparte in Egypt. Nelson found a solution to the vexing problem of how to mass on one part of the enemy's force while containing the rest, a problem that naval theorists had been puzzling over for centuries. In this action, Nelson is credited with instantly perceiving at the critical moment the possibility of an unprecedented maneuver and with initiating it without a moment's hesitation. Dashing in alongside the French ships, he anchored his craft in such a way as to obtain a two-to-one advantage. The effect of the firepower he thus was able to deliver on the French fleet was annihilating.

As a result, the following day saw an unparalleled scene of triumph for the British fleet on the one hand, and of utter devastation for the French fleet on the other. The British had lost some men, but not a single ship, while the French casualties were nearly six times as great, and all of the French ships except three at the rear of the line had been taken or destroyed. While Napoleon's specter was soon to haunt Europe, Nelson's haunted Napoleon from this moment forward. Nelson was an obstacle Napoleon was never able to overcome, even at the height of his power.

Another author, C. J. Britton, in his book *New Chronicles of the Life of Lord Nelson,* makes a statement similar to those made by Mahan, describing intuition as we know it now, but in terms of his day. "In both events [Copenhagen and St. Vincent] he showed the true stamp of leadership by instantly divining the right thing to be done and doing it without the loss of a moment."[4]

When the Battle of Trafalgar loomed, Nelson proved fully equal to it because he possessed genius for war. Mahan remarks:

. . . intellectual faculties, which, though not unsuspected had not previously been allowed scope for their full exercise. Before him was now open a field of possibilities hitherto unexampled in naval warfare; and for the appreciation of them was needed just those perceptions, intuitive in origin, yet resting firmly on well-ordered, rational processes which on the intellectual side distinguished him above all other British seamen.[5]

Nelson's most decisive actions at Trafalgar were not only the result of intuition, particularly that intuitive idea which selected the moment to give the order to close with the French fleet, but also were the result of a series of other shrewd but lesser judgments. He first lulled the enemy into a sense of confidence, and later lured them out of port. Before the battle was closed, he pressed the French fleet closely and relentlessly for a period of time, an intuitive idea that was a major factor in rattling the French admiral. Breaking the French line at Trafalgar, important as a tactic of the battle and conforming with naval principles developed earlier by other naval strategists, in this case was not so important as the intuitive "embracing at the happy moment,"[6] as Mahan calls it, which allowed him to do so.

Possibly taking a lesson from Hawke at Quiberon Bay, the action of Union Admiral David Glasgow Farragut, easily the outstanding Naval commander of the War Between the States, proved surprisingly parallel in similar circumstances. In spite of remonstrances from his most able lieutenant, of further caution from his other officers, and with only the ambiguous instructions of the Navy Department to justify his action, he boldly ran his fleet past the defenses of Vicksburg. Disregarding his less perceptive lieutenants, Farragut showed not only the admirable strategic insight that found successful military solutions, but also the courage that dared to accept on his sole responsibility the immense risk taken as he passed the forts. This strategic insight had previously been demonstrated in New Orleans and later at Mobile Bay, where he also chose to pass by the major defenses, severing their communications to ensure their downfall.

Mahan adds:

For the power to take these momentous decisions, Farragut was indebted to nature. He indeed justified them in his general course of action by good and sufficient reasons, but the reasons carried instant conviction to him because they struck a tender chord in his breast.[7]

The Battle of Jutland in World War I sealed the fate of the German Navy and dashed the Kaiser's desperate hope that the German High Seas Fleet might open the shipping lanes through the North Sea. During this battle, the smoke and haze of the heavy bombardment concealed from the captains the whereabouts of the enemy ships, forcing them to fire almost by instinct. It became quite clear at Jutland that technological developments had undermined traditional naval tactics. Long-range guns, high speeds of operation, and diversity of ship types had not been accompanied by a corresponding extension of the commander's eyesight. At Trafalgar, Nelson had the whole fleet in view for several hours during the slow approach. At Jutland, the opposing fleets sometimes approached each other at express-train speeds, and the commanders had only moments to make decisions based on little or no dependable information.

The conditions described above were such that a high degree of on-the-spot intuitive judgment had to be exercised on both sides. By the time of World War II, the pace of naval action had quickened. New weapons never before employed in warfare — the aircraft carrier, the air fleets of the vast carrier task forces, the new electronic devices that permitted location of an unseen enemy, the tremendous increases in firing power — were but a few of the new things that the naval officer had to learn to use. All these developments had to be coordinated by naval leaders into hard-hitting forces using tactics and techniques never before tried or tested.

The rapidity with which the Navy had to function in the Pacific in World War II and the enormity of the intellectual task confronting the admirals are evident in an action selected from extensive accounts of the war. It is a small part of the devastating Battle of the Philippine Sea, in which the quiet and unassuming Admiral Marc A. Mitscher played a decisive role.

In *The Magnificent Mitscher*, Theodore Taylor writes:

[Admiral Mitscher was] recognized within the Navy as one of the greatest combat officers in the history of air or sea warfare — a nautical Jeb Stuart who hid beneath weather fronts to make his attacks, and was engaged in every major naval battle in the Pacific during World War II except Coral Sea. He fought more naval engagements than Farragut and John Paul Jones combined. He introduced or sponsored most of the intricate tactics used by vast carrier task forces.[8]

At 1540 hours on June 20, 1944, Lieutenant Nelson, a pilot from the aircraft carrier *Enterprise,* sighted a Japanese combat ship.[9]

Admiral Mitscher received, at 1542 hours, the intimation only that Lieutenant Nelson had seen something, somewhere —nobody could make out what, the message was so garbled.[10] A quick decision was wanted, for time was running out; the sun would set at 1900 hours — less than four hours later — darkness would soon follow, and the stretches of the Pacific were no place for a carrier's pilot to be looking for a flight deck.

Mitscher alerted the task force promptly and at 1553 hours informed Admiral Spruance, his superior, that he expected to make an all-out strike, even though recovery of airplanes from his many aircraft carriers must take place after dark. At 1557 hours Admiral Mitscher received Lieutenant Nelson's definite contact report, that the Japanese fleet, spread out in three groups, was heading west at slow speed, apparently fueling. At 1605, eight minutes later, another pilot in Nelson's flight modified the report and gave a more accurate position, placing the nearest enemy group over 275 miles from Task Force 58.[11]

The danger inherent in the decision to strike, and the reasons for making it, cannot be better stated than in Admiral Mitscher's own words:

Taking advantage of this opportunity to destroy the Japanese fleet was going to cost us a great deal in planes and pilots because we were launching at the maximum range of our aircraft at such a time that it would be necessary to recover them after dark. This meant that all carriers would be recovering daylight-trained air groups at night, with consequent loss of some pilots who were not familiar with night landings and who would be fatigued at the end of an extremely hazardous and long mission. Night landings after an attack are slow at best. There are always stragglers who have had to fight their way out of enemy disposition, whose planes are damaged, or who get lost. It was estimated that it would require about four hours to recover planes, during which time the Carrier Task Groups would have to steam upwind or on an easterly course. This course would take us away from the position of the enemy at a high rate. It was realized also that this was a single-shot venture, for planes which were sent out on this late afternoon's strike would probably not all be operational for a morning strike.[12]

However unusual the circumstances and the dangers involved, though alarmingly brief was the time available to make up his mind, Admiral Mitscher did not hesitate. He informed the Commander of the Fifth Fleet that the carriers (Mitscher's) were firing their bolt.[13]

The score: a Japanese carrier sunk and two-thirds of Admiral Ozaka's remaining planes downed. In three minutes, based on the sketchiest of information and guided solely by intuition, Admiral Mitscher made a decision to risk all, and it paid off.

Primarily in the Pacific Theater, where the major sea warfare of World War II was fought, the rapier thrusts of destroyers and destroyer squadrons reached equal pinnacles of achievement. Their high success, among other factors, was the result of the freedom and initiative accorded to their commanders. Admiral Arleigh Burke, whose personal achievements mark him as a great creative artist, was at his best when operating under policies that afforded him maximum freedom. It is worth citing his wartime recollections of his commander, Admiral Halsey, which indicate the environment within which Admiral Burke, a destroyer squadron commander, worked.

Our orders were very elastic as Admiral Halsey's orders usually were. They were good. They gave us leeway to do what was necessary and yet gave us information so that we knew everything that we had to know. We were not tied down by specific things except to attack.[14]

In a recorded statement made after the Battle of Empress Augusta Bay, Admiral Burke emphasizes this point.

Probably there has been no man placed in the responsible position of Task Force Commander who does not desire to hold a check-rein. He knows that the subordinates have neither the knowledge nor information that is available in the Flagship. Yet past action in this and other wars indicates that *successful actions result from the initiative of well indoctrinated subordinates* [Author's italics].[15]

The challenge of the enemy to a captain at sea is compounded twice over by the challenge of the elements of nature, and now, in modern warfare, the immense materiel in ship and firepower that must be manipulated.

Commander Howard Bucknell, U.S.N., sums it up well when he says:

Play your hunches, Captain. No one else in the ship can develop such a composite "feel" for the ship as her captain . . . Many commanding officers have had cause to regret that they did not heed that small inner voice that their unique experience, non-watchkeeping responsibility, and continuing information gave them.[16]

CHAPTER SEVEN

The Cruel and Creative Sea

Commander Sam Dealey had the vision and mind of an artist.

LIEUTENANT LYNCH
USS *Harder*

IT IS A PARADOX of war that the comparatively slow-moving, virtually blind submarine — no match in armament for the average surface warship and energetically hunted by aircraft — nevertheless evaded overwhelming enemy sea power to bring England to the verge of defeat in two world wars and snapped the back of Japan in the second of these conflicts.

Combat reports reveal sub attacks as rapacious, dramatic masterpieces of battle — quickly conceived, tenaciously carried through, and decisively final.

Yet attempts to understand the mysterious quality that makes the submarine terrifying and deadly have proved generally fruitless. The underwater warcraft remains a military enigma whose destructive power promises to be far greater in future wars.

What enables the submarine to be such an effective weapon is not so much the torpedoes and missiles, plus the ultra-modern materiel, but rather the special character of the submarine skipper's intellect and the ideas it spawns. Undersea power, in my opinion, develops from the free, sharply honed, dynamically creative mind of the skipper who sees new and unusual combinations for the total resources at his disposal. These consist of the skilled technicians that man the submarines, the weapons, the physical environment — the surface of the world's oceans and their depths, weather—yes, even the minds of the enemy. The captain's intellect gathers and manipulates all these as his creative talent dictates. It is the creative mind that makes the submarine a devastating weapon.

Creativity in underwater techniques is enhanced by the cultivation and practice of sharpening sense perceptions by looking through periscopes and listening in via sonar carefully and repeatedly to schools of fish, sharks, and man-made deep-water sounds until they become as familiar as sneezes and the striking of a match. This crystallizes knowledge within the intellect and, in turn, produces a high order of creativity by intelligent evaluation through intuitive perception.

The submarine captain is the creative manipulator of his total environment and resources, including the sea, which, as Commander Edward L. Beach mentions, ". . . is the submarine's friend, medium and testor, he embraces eagerly at every opportunity, carefully, and within wholesome respect."[1] This is typical of the creative intellect which molds everything, including elements of its environment, into an idea. The captain ". . . uses the sea and its properties. The effect of bright warm sunlight on it, for example, interests him greatly." [2] High waves can help hide his periscope at

one time, and reveal it dangerously to the enemy at another,
and the captain must know how to use the waves best. The
type of sea bottom is vitally important—for sometimes he
must rest silently on it to avoid detection. "The temperature
of the water, the depth, and the amount of marine life" — the
fish, seaweed, crustacea — "all are of consuming importance." [3] In analyzing the submariner, one is invariably struck
by "his indefinable oneness with, and deep understanding of,
the sea." [4]

The submarine is able to exist for months at sea. It is able
to range far and wide. The captain is rarely spared a moment
for relaxation. He becomes intensely involved with his mission, the mechanical apparatus of his craft, and the intellectual caliber of his crew. His senses sharpen, alert to mes-
sages from either and he gives a quick interpretation to their
meaning. Events and sensual experiences cram facts into his
intellect to make him highly specialized, his intellect well
prepared for an engagement. The closed environment with
constant transfer of orders and responses develops a strong
empathy between captain and crew to enable the crew to
quickly perceive the captain's intuitions or judgments. The
captain is king in his domain, largely unaffected by outside
influence. He has the ideal conditions to become a master in
the art of undersea warfare. Commander Beach has made the
point that "Whatever the state of the individual and of in-
ternal affairs," the submarine "acts under a single directive
force — a single brain — the Captain's." [5] Most American submarine captains have been able to respond well to their circumstance. Other nations have not been so lucky.

Admiral Hall, who commanded the British submarine
service during the greater period of World War I, and the
directing power and conceiver of many ideas which caused

drastic changes to be made in the size and character of British submarines, has stated about captains who command these submarines:

Fortunately, not every nation can produce proper men to command submarines, and if they cannot we can safely let them have as many and as large submarines as they like.[6]

The inference here is that it is men who command, and submarines without proper commanders are useless.

The individual exploits of German U-boats of the two world wars are dramatic. There is hardly an encounter on land, at sea, or in the air that can match the action of September 22, 1914. In just a little over an hour, German Lieutenant Weddigen, captaining 28 men in a 400-ton U-boat, sank the British cruisers *Aboukir, Cressy,* and *Hogue,* displacing 40,000 tons and carrying 2,265 men.

During April, 1917, fifty German submarine commanders sank almost 900,000 tons of shipping. However, most of this terrible destruction was the work of only a few men out of that fifty. It is said that if Germany had been able to pick and train her submarine commanders so that 50 percent of them were efficient instead of about 5 percent, the submarine would have choked off the sea lanes, and the war would have been over in August 1917 because England would have been unable to survive for a lack of food. One British admiral stated that twenty German submarine commanders were responsible for 66 percent of the total losses inflicted on allied and neutral shipping at sea during World War I.

During World War II, some twenty-three years later, in a single attack on the "Night of the Long Knives" (the night of October, 18-19, 1940) German Commander Prien could write on a small pad, "Have sunk eight ships in the convoy totaling 50,500 tons. All torpedoes fired."[7] Many other dramatic undersea actions in World War II were performed in as short a time or less.

Germany, with only eight U-boats at sea in 1939, sank thirty-eight ships in the month of December. She scored a record of sixty-three sinkings in October 1940 with only twelve subs. In the twenty-seven-month period of the Battle of the Atlantic, as Nicholas Monsarrat in *The Cruel Sea* says:

> The tide was now set and running strongly against all allied shipping. It was like a dark stain spreading all over the huge sea; the area of safety diminished, the poisoned water, in which no ship could count on safety from hour to hour, seemed swiftly to infect a wider and wider circle.[8]

U-boats sank 973 Allied ships including the battleship H.M.S. *Royal Oak* and the aircraft carrier H.M.S. *Courageous*. This averaged thirty-six Allied ships sunk a month by an average of fourteen U-boats at sea per month.

Slipping into the Atlantic sea lanes early in 1941 in what was almost a ludicrous plan painfully loaded against the U-boats participating, seven of Germany's undersea craft aggregating about 5,000 tons, carrying a grand total of only 84 torpedoes, and officered and manned by only 308 personnel staggered the Allies. One of these subs, the U-99 under Captain Kretschmer, sank 300,000 tons of Allied shipping; by March three of Germany's early aces, Kretschmer, Prien, and Schepke, sank more than 800,000 tons.

On a rampage under the able hand of Kapitan Hardegen, the German submarine U-123 on the night of January 18, 1942, sank 8 ships totaling 53,360 tons; the U-66 under Kapitanleutnant Kale, 3 tankers and 1 freighter totaling 30,748 tons. In just ten days of action these same U-boats plus others sank 95 ships totaling 200,000 tons. This veritable underwater hurricane prompted a worried Churchill on

February 6, 1942, to send an urgent note to the White House. He called the attention of President Roosevelt to the fact that since January 12 confirmed losses stood at 158,208 tons, and probable losses at another 83,740 tons more; the total, including possible losses, 259,311 tons. On March 12 he again reminded the White House that in the Caribbean Sea some 60 tankers, a staggering loss of 600,000 deadweight tons, had been sunk.

America, alone, in the first year of the war lost 1,027 Allied ships to U-boat action. Before this holocaust was over, the world saw 17,000,000 tons of Allied shipping sunk by German U-boats during World War II. In March 1942 in American waters U-boats sank 74 ships totaling 424,547 tons, with the month of May showing a record of 91 Allied ships going to the bottom, and a total of 519 ships aggregating 2,800,000 tons by July 1942, 90 percent of which took place in the so-called United States strategic area.

The Americans achieved a similar record against Japanese shipping and warships. Although American submarines sank a total of 5,320,094 tons, or one-third the amount the Germans sank, American achievements, by comparison, can be considered formidable. The Germans placed heavy emphasis on the submarine from the very beginning of the war and produced a total of 1,150 U-boats. Most of these went to sea before the war ended.

The United States, by comparison, at the eve of the outbreak of the war had 111 submarines in commission and 73 in building. Of the 51 submarines on duty or available for duty in the Pacific, 29 were attached to the Atlantic Fleet, and 22 operated with the Pacific Fleet. By the end of the war, the Americans had produced a total of 288 submarines, not all of which were used in the Pacific. Only 184 sank 5,320,094 tons of Japanese shipping.

In the year 1944 alone, United States submarines destroyed 8 light cruisers, 28 destroyers, and a number of Japanese submarines. Thus in a single year such a whopping blow was struck that the Japanese Navy was reduced to impotence and, in large measure, the way was paved for the final drive to Tokyo.

Theodore Roscoe states in *United States Submarine Operations in World War II:* "*It was in the third dimension that Japan lost the Pacific war.*"[9] The atom bombs that consumed Hiroshima and Nagasaki could not blind observers to the fact that Japan, by the time those bombs had exploded, was already destroyed.

And Roscoe continues:

And long before the first mass air raids smote Tokyo, many Japanese-held harbors in the southwest Pacific were as deserted as the bays of the moon, and in many of Japan's home seaports there were vacant docks with rusting bollards where only spiders tied their lines. The atomic bomb was a funeral pyre of an enemy who had been drowned.[10]

Fifty-five percent of all Japanese shipping, that is, merchant and naval shipping, downed in World War II was sunk by United States submarines. This is an achievement the stupendous nature of which is comprehended only when it is realized that a mere 2 percent of the United States naval personnel, or a force that averaged 14,750 officers and men, was responsible for this accomplishment.

The following is a firsthand account of the sinking of the Japanese ship the *Osama Maru* by the USS *Atule* taken from the "Report of War Patrol Number One, USS *Atule* (SS 403)," U.S. Naval Archives and an interview with Admiral J. H. Maurer, then commanding officer of the *Atule*. It is appropriate for the manner in which it highlights some of the major aspects of creativity.

At 0238 1 November 1944, after having dived to prevent being observed by an enemy aircraft sighted earlier, I surfaced the *Atule*. Soon my radar spotted a huge form some distance out. I headed towards it to come to a normal approach. We closed in to about 17,000 yards.

At about 0325 I made my first contact on the first escort guarding my quarry. At 0331 I contacted the second escort. A few minutes later the target at 1300 was in eyesight, the leading escort at 5000. Occasional squalls occurred.

At 0359, I ordered battle stations torpedo. The escorts were closing in.[11]

He elaborated in the interview:

As I maneuvered the *Atule* more deeply into the course of the oncoming convoy, I realized that the time for decision loomed; our situation was becoming increasingly dangerous and I had to make up my mind immediately. I had three courses open to me. I could turn out of the path of the oncoming patrol craft and my target, I could submerge, or I could bore into the screen of escorts and through the target. I decided it was now or never. I was losing true bearing rapidly. I reacted instantaneously. All my being told me without hesitation I must go on in fast. I would lose my impetus—lose it completely—if I submerged or turned away. It was a tense moment. I knew in a flash I was right! I knew that if I was to be successful it was the only course of action to take. If I turned or dove I would lose my opportunity forever. As it turned out I had to pick the course of action taken—there was no other.

In retrospect, my judgment told me the situation was untenable, I was in the midst of a convoy. My situation was extremely critical. The logical thing to have done would have been to get out of harm's way, but my intuition told me differently. It told me we're here, we've got everything in suitable condition to attack.[12]

The report continues:

At 0359 all ships were in sight of the naked eye.... It was bright as hell. The target—very large passenger type—single funnel. Number two escort on port quarter target.

At 0432 commenced firing six torpedoes, depth ten feet across heavy sea. Could see details on all ships but weren't much interested....

0434 — terrific explosion at middle of target — threw flaming material three times higher than mast. Range to escort No. 3 (on target starboard quarter) 1200.

Decided to get out of sight; second explosion as I left the bridge. Three torpedo explosions heard in forward torpedo room, two in control room, conning tower and bridge.

0440 — nine depth charges, none close.

0545 — very loud and heavy cracking and breaking up noises heard throughout the ship in the direction of the target.[13]

Admiral Maurer stated in the interview, "after the attack I sensed an exhilaration — a feeling of release."[14]

Commander Beach in *Submarine* describes the racing moments when the radar operator of the USS *Batfish* on February 9, 1944, in the Babuyan Channel south of Camiguin Island noticed something out of the ordinary: ". . . a faint shimmer of the scope — a momentary unsteadiness in the green and amber cathode-ray tubes — which comes and goes...."[15] And then the message, " 'Captain to conn [conning tower],' "[16] shot to his captain just getting a moment of shut-eye. In a moment the captain was in the conning tower. " 'There it is, sir! There it is again! I just noticed it a minute ago!' "[17] the operator tells his captain. "The captain stares at the instrument, weighing the meaning of what he sees. This is something new, something portentous — there is a small stirring in the back of his mind — there seems to be a half-remembered idea there, if he can only dig it up — then, like a flash, he has it!" "Japanese submarine!"[18] This conclusion, arrived at in seconds, was highly intuitive and tripped off a series of closely related intellectual responses that terminated in the torpedoing of the enemy sub.

Describing the action of Commander J. W. Blanchard of the USS *Albacore*, when it made its attack against an immense Japanese aircraft carrier, Commander Beach again gives some inkling of the speed with which decisions had to be made.

Blanchard has had about ten seconds to figure all this out. He cannot wait longer. The risks, the odds, all facets of what he is about to do flash through his mind. This is a desperate chance he is about to take, and he is putting his ship and his fine loyal crew into grave danger. The carrier, and all that that ship might mean to other United States forces — Jim [Blanchard] must make the decision alone, without help, and instantly.[19]

Probably the most legendary underwater nemesis to Japan's fleet was Commander Sam Dealey of the USS *Harder*. In *Through Hell and Deep Water* Admiral Charles Lockwood, who knew Sam Dealey intimately, relates:

. . . what made Dealey such an outstanding success as a combat skipper was not primarily his absolute fearlessness but his amazing ability to make instant and correct decisions. Where others might have hesitated—held off for better evaluation or a bit more data—Dealey instantly bored into the attack with seemingly instinctive knowledge of how it should be done.[20]

Of Sam Dealey, the Admiral continues:

. . . perusal of Sam's own log produces ample evidence of his initiative and keen analytical talent. He seldom failed to get directly to the heart of a puzzling situation or an unusual attack setup, and his handling of torpedo firing problems was nothing short of uncanny.[21]

This last talent, according to a member of the crew of the

Harder, stemmed from Dealey's remarkable visual sense.

He [Dealey] had the mind of an artist. His imagination pictured situations so vividly and scenes photographed themselves so clearly on the retina of his mind that he really did not need a TDC [Torpedo Direction Computer] solution for making his attacks.[22]

Let me give an example of what Commander Dealey's mind could do for him in an emergency. The submerged *Harder* lay in front of three important targets steaming almost abreast, driving straight toward the *Harder.* At 0537, Dealey fired three torpedoes from the bow tubes at the right flank ship. Then with the forward tube he fired three torpedoes at the center ship at the almost point-blank range of 600 yards. Admiral Lockwood described it:

. . . [the action of his encounter was] almost too swift for the mind to follow, and the *Harder's* position at this time, as well as her life expectancy, might optimistically be described as most insecure. There she was, with torpedo hits being registered from six torpedoes she had just fired (at two different ships) in mortal peril of being rammed by another ship or blown to bits by the depth charges of a vengeful destroyer close at hand. Swift action was required.[23]

Dealey's patrol log from this point onward reads as follows:

0538 — Swung hard to right to prevent being rammed by left flank AK. [At this time he heard two hits on his first target and three on his second.]

0542— Fired three stern tube shots: track angle 120 port; two range was too close and the gyro too large, 136 degrees. Continued swinging wide and shifted back to the center AK. He had turned left again, presented a perfect target at 1500 yards.

0542—Fired three stern tube shots: track angle 120 port; two hits! This has been a dream come true. The *Harder* was in the middle of an enemy convoy and I [Sam Dealey] felt like a possum in a henhouse, but the destroyer escorts were uninvited

participants. . . . The reconstructed melee is only an approxima-
tion at best; screw noises in every direction, torpedo explosions,
a near collision, and then the destroyers started dropping depth
charges![24]

Admiral Lockwood writes:

In *five* terrific action-packed minutes, the *Harder* had fired ten
torpedoes at *three* different targets and obtained *seven* hits. One
ship sank with five hits in her; one limped away suffering from
two hits; and a third still had a whole skin. Not a single fish
[torpedo] remained in the *Harder's* tubes.[25]

In another equally incredible action, Commander Dealey,
observing two enemy destroyers, decided to attack, but his
intuition told him to withhold the attack until the two
destroyers positioned themselves ideally for a torpedo launch
— a submariner's dream. The result: Two destroyers sunk by
a single torpedo spread all in a period of about nine minutes
from the time of sighting the destroyers until they had nosed
to the ocean's depths. As reported in Roscoe's book *Submarine:* Ten minutes after opening fire, Commander Dealey
"surfaced to allow others to see the damage and to make
rapid shift to a more quiet neighborhood."[26] Nothing could
be seen in the bright moonlight except a large quantity of
steam and vapor over the spot of the first sinking and a light
buoy burning where the second destroyer had been. The
destroyer that had been vaporized was the Imperial Navy's
Tanikaze. In a period of three days, the *Harder* was credited
with sinking three enemy destroyers.

The strategic consequences of the violent antidestroyer
drives launched by the *Harder* could not be measured alone
in tons sunk, or in the destroyers it removed. The effect of
these new tactics is reported to have so alarmed the Japanese
that they were forced to devise a new concept of warfare,
causing Admiral Ozawa to delay his carrier force in the

Philippine Sea, with disastrous results.

While this discussion is primarily on the subject of submarine attack, there is no question that a high order of intuition developed among submarine captains attempting to evade depth charges launched by attacking enemy surface and aircraft. The USS *Trigger,* after one attack and a dive at 300 feet, had 25 depth charges dropped on her. Her steel sides buckled in and out; cork insulation on the interior broke off and flew in great chunks. Ventilation lines and other piping vibrated, light sheet metal seams and fastenings popped loose. The ship jiggled violently. Electrical instruments were shattered and electrical circuits thrown out of order. While this was going on, five more escort destroyers sought out the *Trigger,* joining the sixth to form a ring circling their prey. No matter which way the *Trigger* turned, the destroyers kept her within the circle. Every hour one would break off from the circle and make the run, dropping more charges. For seventeen hours the *Trigger* crept and cringed under continual harassment. No matter which way the *Trigger* went the circle hovered ominously above. Hours later, finally, heading for the biggest gap in the circle, the *Trigger* slowly increased speed. Commander Beach described the event:

We listened with bated breath, hardly daring to breathe, plotting in those malevolent screws, trying to identify the bird who was supposed to cover the sector we had chosen for our escape route. Here he comes! One set of screw noises slowly gets louder and begins to draw ahead. We shudder as it gains bearing on us. Surely he'll pick us up, because he'll be practically right on top of us! But—another smile from the blindfolded gal—all at once he stops drawing ahead. Now, as we cluster around the sound gear, we watch the tell-tale bearing pointer moving aft, ever aft, 'til finally he passes across our stern! A guarded cheer breaks from the desperate men in the conning tower. We've broken through.[27]

Sliding out from Pearl Harbor on March 3, 1945, late in the war for the average submarine, the USS *Tirante* compiled an enviable record. In fifty-two days she attacked twelve enemy vessels, downed six, shot up the rest, and raised a Yellow Sea storm that "snarled up the Japanese transportation," as Theodore Roscoe describes it in *United States Submarine Operations in World War II*, "to Seoul, Darien, Tientsin and Tsingtao."[28]

Commander G. L. Street, captain of the *Tirante*, envisioned he would have more luck if he hunted where the Japanese would not expect an inquisitive periscope. After careful analysis, he reached the conclusion that the Japanese ships were following evasive routes along shallow coastal waters heretofore unexplored by submarines. Although his independent action was sanctioned by Fleet Headquarters he devised his strategy independently. To these shallow waters he took the *Tirante*. A résumé of his actions in an attack made soon after entering this area, taken from a citation that ultimately resulted in a Congressional Medal of Honor for Commander Street, said that he demonstrated extreme aggressiveness, brilliant planning, and daring. The commanding officer

. . . took his submarine deep into the enemy's inner defenses in a meticulous search for enemy shipping. With sagacity and consummate skill, he penetrated strong escort screens in the shallow water and thereafter launched four devastating torpedo attacks that resulted in the sinking of three ships, one of which was a 500-ton transport loaded with troops. At that point, after withstanding a severe depth charging attack, the gallant submarine bounded back with a vengeance and launched a brilliantly executed torpedo attack to sink a valuable 1500-ton patrol vessel. In the confusion following the sinking, the *Tirante* skillfully made her escape.[29]

The report commends his deed as the result of "sound deductions and brilliant reasoning."[30]

Later, Commander Street determined that enemy ships were using a confined harbor on the north shore of Quelpart for an anchorage. To reach this anchorage, he had to take his submarine through many miles of shallow water in which his ship would not be able to dive. The harbor was inevitably mined, many reefs and shoals were known to exist, and the whole area was closely guarded by shore-based radar, numerous patrol vessels, and extensive air coverage. In spite of the monumental dangers ahead, Street ordered "battle stations. Torpedo." Thereafter some rapid maneuvers torpedoed a nearby 10,000-ton tanker, from which, when hit, a great mushroom of white blinding flames shot 3,000 feet into the air, the thunderous roar nearly flattening the crew of the *Tirante*. In the light of the burning tanker, two new Mikura-class frigates spotted the *Tirante* and started in for the kill. Quickly bringing his submarine to bear on the leading frigate, the commanding officer tenaciously fired two do-or-die torpedoes at the vessel which was endeavoring to block his escape, and then swung his ship and fired his last torpedo at the other frigate.

With all torpedoes expended, Commander Street headed his submarine out of the confined harbor at full speed, just as the torpedoes hit the first frigate and blew it sky-high. Seconds later, the sister ship disintegrated.

If one is to judge the validity of theory by the results of its practical application, the case for intuition at sea rests, handsomely supported by the authentic action accounts weighted by the hulks of more than 26,000,000 tons of world shipping collecting barnacles on the ocean floors of the globe — a mute testimonial to the naval captain's creative intellect successfully at work in war.

CHAPTER EIGHT

Creativity and the Leadership Task

The challenge of creativity is to walk down a lonely road unafraid.

ANONYMOUS

Great men are like eagles and build their nests in solitude.

SCHOPENHAUER

SOME THOUGHTS on creativity have been expressed by Schopenhauer, Tolstoi, Bergson, Carlyle, James, Sorel, and other philosophers. More recently, authorities from other disciplines have become interested in this subject. In the early 1950's, Professor J. P. Guilford of the University of Southern California noticed its neglect by psychologists. Alarmed, he was instrumental in stimulating the development of the creative education movement in the United States, a movement that has swelled to such dimensions in recent years that he was prompted to remark that it "seems to be headed for something of enormous benefit to humanity."[1]

The National Science Foundation, the University of Buffalo, and the University of Southern California have done notable work in the field of creativity. More than one hundred projects probing into various aspects of the subject have been undertaken in the past few years by both private and governmental agencies. Furthermore, industry has shown interest, with General Motors, Dow Chemical, and General Electric moving into the field aggressively, aware of the financial potential available through accelerating the creativity of the individuals who make up the industrial empires.

It is apparent that the preponderant effort in realizing the potential of creativity is logically in the field of education; however, industry and the professions are gradually showing a growing interest.

Harold H. Anderson in *How to Think Creatively* asks for a broadening of interest in creativity and the application of knowledge on the subject to national problems as a social need not restricted to the narrow investigations being conducted. He made the point that creativity is a matter of national survival, and warned that lack of creativity is ". . . a national crisis, a desperate situation for military forces, for industrial leadership and for humanitarian living."[2]

The more recent American interest in the subject of creativity and the spate of associated research activity is by no means purely accidental, the efforts of Professor Guilford and the prophetic and cautionary advice of Hutchinson notwithstanding. Interest in these concepts was accelerated by the first Soviet satellite, when a humiliated America tardily awakened and rose in challenge.

This enormous achievement, coming from a seemingly less advanced nation, caused our politicians to raise some serious questions as to the quality of our education versus that of the Soviets. Subsequently, heroic measures have been taken to improve the quality of our education and to expand curricula to give the United States the necessary technical and scientific skills, and to press our students to greater effort. Some educators began working concurrently in the direction of seeing what could be done to get more brainpower from existing resources to aid in bringing America ahead of the Soviet Union in the space race.

Authorities hold that, if, as is claimed by the proponents of creativity, some of man's greatest technical advancements have come from ideas produced by highly creative types, then sound reasoning dictates that it is now a matter of national urgency, if this concept is valid, that all aspects of creativity must be understood and exploited in the national interest. As a result, the study of the function of man's intellect, and more so, the attempt at understanding the generation of creative ideas, long the realm of the philosopher, are now being vigorously explored. Several years ago, it was suggested that if our creative intellects were properly exploited and our new crop of students was encouraged to expand its creative resources, the total intellectual performance of the United States would be so impressively raised in quantity and quality that it would easily overcome the Russian advantage in the space race.

While creativity is vitally important in attempting to gain the lead in the space environment, our military leadership cannot escape its implications nor can it shirk the responsibility for disregarding the benefits which a knowledge of creativity portends for the future military strength of the nation.

Wars are traditionally fought with weapons and tactics of previous wars to which, for various reasons, commanders find themselves harnessed. Some of these old weapons and tactics have withstood the challenging applications to new conditions through successive wars. The French 75 mm gun was a mainstay through several wars. The bow and arrow is still a favorite even in the modern weapon arsenal where men fight silent warfare. Napoleon's favorite tactic of applying mass against weakness has constantly been reapplied. However, whereas military men in the past have had to contend with the applications of relatively few, if any, new weapons or tactics in the planning for and fighting of a next war, the situation confronting military men now is totally different. Since World War II science and technology have brought into being for the combat commander untried weapons and weapons systems of superlative destructive power whose use can only be conjectured.

Moreover, added to the arsenal of weapons is a host of electronic and mechanical contrivances that proliferate the destructive means to an extent that the combat commander has a formidable task planning and managing their proper use. Man is faced with the awesome task of handling weapons of violence and diversity such as he has never before handled, and with virtually no experience to draw upon. Never has there been a comparable situation between any two wars.

While operations research will be able to provide some sound answers to applications of weapons to wars of the future and to the development of new tactics, the best guarantee to their successful use will be that there are creative men in combat-command positions, who can stand on their own two feet and think brilliantly in terms of the application of total resources.

For the first time in history, it must be recognized that combat commanders will be forced to innovate even in the most mundane encounters. Hence it is essential to define steps that must be taken now to apply our knowledge on intuition and creativity in combat.

The situation in which the professional finds himself today

resembles to a degree a situation in which many eminent leaders have found themselves when they have made breakthroughs. There is a wealth of new materials to work and manipulate, and a daring man, unafraid of the new and unusual that he can create, will forge ahead of the rank-and-file performer to become the successful leader.

The battlefield environment as a whole is conducive to creativity. However, man becomes the essential ingredient in this environment, for without him to react to it and to manipulate it, the environment is meaningless. Thus, a useful discussion must necessarily include an amplification of some points already covered on both subjects — environment and man.

The battlefield gives back to man certain of his freedoms. Upon it many of the laws of his own country become inapplicable, if not meaningless. Take a simple illustration. If a soldier is a jeep driver in a nation at war he is not restricted to driving on the right side of the road unless he meets a vehicle coming from the opposite direction when, by force of habit in order to avoid a crash rather than the excoriation of the law, he may move over to the right. Furthermore, there is no restriction on speed, and if danger arises to make it necessary, he exceeds local speed limits, turns off the road, rips fence wires, and moves across tilled farmland. All these acts he would not practice in an organized community where there is no war, for fear of arrest.

The prerogatives of troops attacking a city, before the civil affairs and military government authorities step in to regulate their behavior with regard to the use of facilities, also follow liberal patterns. Whereas, in his own country no soldier doing his duty would break into a private home without a search warrant, he feels quite free to do otherwise in combat, where it is frequently necessary to break into private homes to seek out snipers or enemy sympathizers. While there may be some ground rules established by the commanders, and there may be other prohibitions, nevertheless troops do not hesitate to bed down in the comfort of such homes in combat areas. Picture troops taking the same liberties in their own communities in the United States!

Then, also, there is the matter of the use and treatment of women. Their presence in a hostile environment is one of the factors most destructive to the continuation of law and order. Conditioned by the moral and ethical cultural level of the invading troops, there will be some normal cohabitation as a minimum, to the extreme of violation and rape. Depending on the level of civilization of an invader, or putting it another way, the level of civilization to which the morality of the invader has deteriorated, he will, under the pragmatic morality that "to the victor belong the spoils," pillage and gather spoils to which he would never be entitled by law or custom in his own country.

The ultimate blow to standard patterns of morality and law comes when he violates, or is told he now has the authority to violate, the commandment "Thou shall not kill," and is told that he shall kill and that it is moral to do so.

Man in war, through these various acts, becomes decivilized, retrogressing in humanity and growing in barbarity as the threat of law recedes. At the same time that this threat of law lessens, the very conditions for a greater freedom for man develop, reaching optimum proportions in the heat of combat.

In other words, as conventional restrictions decrease, frustration diminishes and a soldier's freedom to achieve original and creative action increases. Given these special circumstances, the creative military leader can originate and use ingenious techniques to achieve successful combat operations. This experience can serve his nation positively as he experiences the exhilaration of an artist in the act of creation.

Consequently, one comes to the distasteful but realistic conclusion that war, in the release from law that it allows and in the emotional release that soldiers experience, provides freedom and ideal conditions for the creatively inclined. However, the important point is that this ideal environment for creativity and the suitable preparation of soldiers in this environment for a large number of creative ideas and their implementation have never been scientifically exploited in combat. There are several reasons for this.

First, there has never been an explanation or even a modest understanding of a war environment as a creative one. The previous discussion should be adequate for this purpose. Second is the abysmal lack of understanding of the dynamic, intuitive, highly responsive "dynamic" type "B" creativity on the part of the military man. Third is the problem of how to make soldiers aware of their own creativity, how it could and will work in combat, and, finally, how they should exploit it.

In combat, most men, be they leaders or be they followers, find themselves very frequently alone, faced with the need to come out from under a problem with a solution, even so simple a one as the direction in which to point a gun and squeeze the trigger, or how to abolish an offensive enemy position. When man is alone with these problems, unable to call upon a comrade to exchange ideas, or where, as a commander, none of his staff is there to advise him, he is forced to get his ideas alone. This is a normal situation for the average man in combat. His education and military training will stand him in good stead; the processes of deductive analysis that he has been taught may lead his mind in an orderly fashion to a solution; the application of many of the newly invented techniques for the generation of creativity may prove of some value, but on the whole he will act fundamentally as man has always acted under stress — creatively or stupidly.

In recent years dynamic creativity has been fairly well synthesized. It essentially progresses to a useful idea through a developmental process as follows:

1. Preparation (getting the background information).
2. Incubation (letting the information digest and develop).
3. Inspiration (the spontaneous flash of light).
4. Communication.
5. Verification.

1. *Preparation.* This may be a long, or a brief and intense, experience. Alexander's preparation for leadership is an excellent example. The intellectual development of Napoleon, Patton, MacArthur, and many other leaders compares favorably with Alexander's. Napoleon and Patton were voracious readers. Most great captains have marched to the battlefield, intellects well fortified with the ingredients of knowledge essential to the demands of the great tasks ahead, their minds like Nelson's, as described by Mahan, ready to "open a field of possibilities hitherto unexampled to naval warfare and to whose appreciation of these possibilities was available just the type of perceptions, 'intuitive in origin' yet resting firmly on well-ordered rational processes."[3]

Frazier Hunt in his book *The Untold Story of Douglas MacArthur* relates a story showing MacArthur's similar mental preparation for his tasks.

After MacArthur had taken over command in the Philippines, his adjutant general presented him with a thick, bound volume of mimeographed sheets, explaining with some measure of pride that the Command Staff had gathered a collection of all the precedents that had been established by various commanders so that MacArthur would know what he ought to do no matter what the problem might be.

"We thought you might be interested in having this," the officer explained proudly.

General MacArthur lifted the bulky volume. "It is a tremendous job you have done," he said. "How many copies of this are there exactly?"

"Exactly six, sir," the officer announced.

MacArthur looked him straight in the eye and there was no smile showing when he said, "Well, you get all those six copies together and burn them — every one of them. I'll not be bound by precedents. Any time a problem comes up, I'll make the decision at once — immediately."[4]

Nelson never became hidebound, and MacArthur also refused to be; they stood head and shoulders above their contemporaries, ready to use their well equipped intellects as great wielders of weapons.

While the education and experience of a leader's lifetime provide him with creative ideas for the longer-term problems as well as the immediate ones, solution of the short-term problems usually revolves around the absorption of information involved in the immediate problem itself. For example, if the problem is a stubborn enemy machine-gun nest, the mind of the commander involved with its liquidation has two immediate sources from which to form an intuitive or otherwise creative idea. First, he considers information that has been stored in the particular war. This includes the peculiarities of the enemy: his strengths, his weaknesses, the caliber of his guns, their ranges, the type of terrain, and the peculiarities of the weather. Second, he begins to store information on the problem at hand. He may ponder minutes, hours, or days. In the process, his mind absorbs such additional information as the number of enemy, how tired they are, their brand of courage, the number of guns, the avenues of attack, plus a host of other factors, including what his own resources are that he can use to attack. As a result of this intensive period of preparation, his mind will turn up some idea. Many times it will be in the form of a hunch — an intuitive idea. Staffs will speed up the commander's intellectual intake and give him a better and quicker feel of broader problems. When a commander is of lower rank and without a staff, the information inflow is slower, since its collection is dependent on his individual effort.

2. *Incubation.* The mind absorbs various experiences over a period of time. Many of the experiences and absorbed information may relate to a particular problem confronting the individual. The ideas lie fallow and, as the process is described, "incubate." This incubation time may vary in extent, and then, as the pressure for the solution of a particular problem develops, these bits of knowledge become agitated in a way that can compare with the increase of activity of atoms under the stimulus of heat. Suddenly two of these ideas in which there is a likeness collide and the two, different as they are, fuse to produce a single concept that becomes the intuitive thought and solution to the problem at hand.

While it is desirable for knowledge to lie fallow for periods of time before the mind is ready to produce an intuitive or creative product from it, it is suggested from evidence from combat that the mind can produce creativity with quickness, and the quality of the creative product may, in fact, be improved under the stress of danger. This is a fact borne out in an observation made by Commander Beach: "An individual who never made much of an impression before might rise to astonishing heights of effectiveness under the stimulus of extreme danger."[5] I would also cite heroism under fire as an act frequently born of an idea the mind produces to protect the body in the presence of danger.

3. *Inspiration.* This is a sudden illumination, a flash of insight, the intuition, the hunch — all terms used to describe the birth of an intuitionally creative idea.

4. *Communication.* Between the inspirational message and the final act of verification, however, there is something more required — a communication bridge. To the military leader it is the key which gives the idea the sinew to succeed.

Eugene E. Jennings makes an illuminating observation concerning communication in *Anatomy of Leadership:*

> The leader is more likely to be above the average of the group in intelligence, but not too much so. Communication seems to be a factor in explaining this. The average person may find it difficult to understand the vocabulary employed by those of superior intelligence. On the other hand, individuals of superior intelligence may find it difficult or may not be motivated to express themselves in the manner necessary to acquire leadership.[6]

Communication is the bridge that transmits or makes transmissible the idea from the intellect of the *leader* to the doers — his staff, his commanders, his troops — and to the civilian population he controls or the politicians and diplomats he must influence.

Communication requires a created idea grown to maturity in the mind of the leader and in a form that can be verbalized so that he can express it when the time is ripe. Next, the idea must be expressed in some manner. Unexpressed and uncommunicated, a creative idea, no matter how brilliant, is absolutely worthless. Literature is crammed with the ghosts of would-be authors whose unexpressed words we will never know or hear, who had a good story and never told it. Voice, pen, or typewriter can put the idea respectively to ear or paper, but it must be worked and shaped into a message that is stated in terms and images that the audience, be it a general staff officer, a commander, or the troops, can understand. If this transition is accomplished, then the idea is transmissible. If the message does not have this quality, then the leader's idea is of no consequence, since it will either not be acted upon at all, or at best imperfectly. Occasionally, of course, no words need be spoken when an arm motions the skirmishers to attack.

Last, then, the idea must have someone who can receive it, an audience — in the case of the military leader, a staff officer or officers, or a subordinate commander — and troops to carry out the bidding to its artistic conclusion. Nor can the audience be just any audience. It must have certain qualities. It must be educated to the degree necessary to understand the words or images the message conveys so that its members are able to understand it. The idea must be presented to them at some time before they are to follow its order so that they can absorb it. They must be receptive to the idea, or they must be made receptive to it. For this purpose, the leader has various devices at his disposal. Thorough prior training and military discipline help to make the receiver receptive and amenable.

Most great leaders have in one way or another demonstrated great skill in the ability to communicate, and have been careful that what they intended to communicate, if it was in writing, was clear, complete, and at the inellectual level of those who were to receive the message. While General Grant is criticized for his unimaginative tactics, nevertheless, if the legend is true, he did understand this value of communication. Asked why he kept a particularly and notoriously dull officer on his staff, he is reputed to have remarked to the effect that when he had prepared an order, it was his practice to turn it over to the officer under criticism to read. If that officer was able to understand it, then, Grant felt, it could be understood by anyone in his command.

The importance of communication can be illustrated by turning to the visual arts. For example, a man may well be able to create a painting, but the question is: "Will it sell?" This question is resolved in the marketplace. Is there some part of the public or some individual who sees the painting, who finds the painting interesting, the hues or the paints appealing, or the theme attractive? If the answer is "Yes," he will sell his painting and the picture may well be considered a work of art and the painter an artist, for he communicated. There was an understanding and an acceptance — the purchase.

There are some decisions that will excite the soldiers while other decisions fall flat. Sometimes the commander can force the latter to a conclusion by threat or other means, but the results in this case are usually commensurate. But there are the decisions that to the soldier who must do the deed, have the right "feel." They make him tingle from head to toe. With these, the situation is "*Go!*" The leader who can produce decisions that communicate easily from his pool of intellectual resources has a much easier time of command. Like a true artist, he has established *communication,* and his men will die for him. All great captains have had this knack of producing ideas that established communication with their men.

In most service manuals on military leadership and in the preaching of experienced commanders will be found the dictum: "Know your men." Although there is a clear recognition of the importance of a leader knowing his men, and a great deal of stress is placed on the fact that officers and noncommissioned ranks should strive for this objective, the reason why this is important has rarely been presented with any logic to support it.

True, it is important to know individual men and the talents of each when one wants a particular mission accomplished. It is important to know which company or ship has the best men as a group so as to select a particular skill to fit a special mission; it is well to know which company has the best individual leader or which division should be selected for a unique assignment because of its élan or the leadership of its general. However, it is suggested that the relationship of communication to creativity provides the primary reason why a commander should know his men. The most important reason for knowing one's men, for visiting them frequently on the battlefield or on shipboard, for inspecting them, for conducting the multitude of activities wherein a commander gets to know his men, is that through these activities the commander can better communicate his ideas to them to accomplish the very objective that an artist accomplishes when he achieves a work that touches the soul of his audience.

To communicate with his officers and men a leader must have certain vital military knowledge and skills. He must know his strategy and tactics. An education in strategy and tactics is important from the standpoint that it gives to its possessor certain tested principles to apply, but it is more important to communicate in primarily familiar terms of words and concepts — terms with which officers and men are equally familiar. A leader, to communicate, must be thoroughly schooled in the use of the weapons at his command and their technical capabilities. He must be thoroughly acquainted with his organization and the personalities and abilities of the men in charge of subordinate units. To some of these it is necessary to convey an idea in one way, to others, in yet another; some will be quick to pick up the idea, others may need cajoling or patience and understanding. A leader must, of course, speak a common language deriving from a common cultural and professional environment.

Taken from the standpoint of the soldier or the junior officer who must receive orders from a leader, there are certain necessary essentials that must exist. As with the officer, this junior must be familiar with the environment in which he is located. He must also have a knowledge of war — not necessarily as sophisticated or complete a knowledge as the leader issuing the order, but enough to understand the order, the terms in which it is couched, the weapons he must use, and the enemy whereof it speaks.

The *Manual of Naval Tactics* states it well:

It is of little avail that Admirals are accomplished tacticians, unless subordinates, especially captains, understand the system familiarly, so as to, at once, comprehend a manoeuvre directed by signal. . . . This readiness cannot be suddenly acquired.[7]

Communication perhaps is impossible because, as often is the case, subordinate minds are chained in the irons of tradition, and this has proved frustrating or disastrous to commanders with supple and creative minds. So it was with John Paul Jones, who never fought by the book, and who, alert to profit by opportunities, found that his ideas were too unusual to be comprehended by his junior officers. In fact, the more imaginative and dashing the commander the less chance he has of being followed and obeyed. The French Admiral Bailly de Suffern was never able to obtain the proper cooperation in his Indian Ocean operations for the simple reason that, although his new strategy and tactics were brilliant, the principles were contrary to those accepted for the day. Consequently, his lieutenants supported him inadequately in the hour of need.

Gabriel Darrieus in *War on the Sea* thought the error in part to be de Suffern's and supports the point made earlier on the importance of communication. Here, communication of the artist's idea, so important to its success, may have failed since, although de Suffern had the "making of an incomparable tactician because he felt the necessity of revolutionizing maneuvers which were too much regulated, and too confined,"[8] he did not take the trouble to explain his plans to his lieutenants before battle. This may explain "the persistence with which those captains held back from full cooperation,"[9] to ultimately compromise his success.

Dissemination of ideas through various news media such as company, ship, or squadron bulletins or newspapers, by the posting of certain memoranda on bulletin boards, and by information programs offer other possibilities. However good the creative idea alone may be, the battalions, no matter how courageous they are, no matter how well trained they may be, will be ineffective at the critical time unless the leader has established effective communication so that the idea can be grasped properly.

5. *Verification.* Alexander's victorious battles verified his brilliant ideas. Napoleon verified his at countless decisive victories. Running the shoals at Quiberon Bay, Hawke verified his idea. MacArthur made his Inchon landing. Verification is an essential conclusion to the creative process.

CHAPTER NINE

Creativity—
The Crux of Leadership

> . . . and the tactical instincts that serve to gain small victories may always be expanded into the winning of great ones with suitable opportunity; because in human affairs the sources of success are ever to be found in the fountains of quick resolve and the swift stroke.
>
> JOHN PAUL JONES

THE GREAT CREATIVE CAPTAINS of history are a notoriously unharmonious group intellectually and physically except in their emission of a stream of new, dynamic ideas. The few serious studies that have applied the usual standards by which ability has been measured in other fields have not arrived at very conclusive results; no satisfying universal answers are yet available to show how these unique individuals have, *as a group*, been successful. If these facts were known, a set of criteria could be established by the armed services and employed in the selection of personnel who demonstrate these creative capabilities.

Warfare's greatest leaders do not conform to any discernible pattern, nor is it possible to aggregate them into a number of identifiable groups. Their intelligence does not appear to be uniformly high. General Douglas MacArthur graduated at the top of his class at West Point. Plutarch, in writing about Alexander the Great, leaves us with the impression that Alexander had a brilliant mind, and says the same about Caesar. Not only was Caesar a genius as an orator and statesman, but Plutarch tells us he was the first to contrive the means for communicating with friends by cipher, when either press of business or the pace of his military activities left him no time for personal conferences. Caesar dictated letters from horseback, and gave directions to two men who took notes at the same time.

In contrast to MacArthur, Alexander, and Caesar, Napoleon lacked brilliance in the academic sense, as his school records show. He excelled in mathematics but showed only ordinary ability in most of the other subjects.

In the Civil War, Generals George Armstrong Custer and George Pickett, staunch hero of the charge across the fields of Gettysburg, were each last in their respective classes at West Point. Several of our most successful generals in World War II were in the lowest academic 10 percent. It took General George Patton five years to complete the four-year course, finally graduating 46th in a class of 103 cadets.[1]

Theodore Taylor in *The Magnificent Mitscher* describes the enigmatic Admiral Mitscher's leadership ability:

. . . it was so deeply buried that nothing short of smelting and remodeling would bring it out. There was no indication of social polish which would enable him to carry out the qualifying diplomatic duties required of a flag officer, and he was only a few places away from "anchor man" [the bottom of the class at the U.S. Naval Academy]. Of course, there had been an earlier "wooden" graduate named William "Bull" Halsey. Scholastic records, Mitscher and Halsey proved, are not always reliable indications of military ability.[2]

Educational background, like intelligence, does not appear to be uniformly high or an important criterion among these men. Philip of Macedon arranged for Aristotle to tutor his son Alexander, and throughout his lifetime Alexander retained a passion for learning. Hannibal shunned a formal education for the rugged, strenuous, physical life. Later, however, he attempted self-education and, as he grew older, he brought into his circle philosophers, scholars, and scientists in whose learning he showed deep interest and understanding. Some of Napoleon's marshals had a fair measure of civilian education, but few had a formal military education except in the practical school of war.

The War Between the States produced some uneducated but able leaders such as Confederate General Nathan Bedford Forrest, scourge of the Union armies in the West. Son of a blacksmith, his childhood, youth, and early manhood were spent amid the wild scenes of the American frontier. This famous soldier had been reared to such hard labor in the struggle for existence that even the scantiest opportunities for an education were denied him.

A study of prominent military leaders shows that many had a remarkable lack of military tradition and education in their backgrounds. Alexander the Great, well educated by Aristotle, trained to ride, hunt, and withstand bodily rigors, nevertheless had little military experience prior to becoming King of Macedonia. Caesar was an orator, politician, and statesman but certainly no military martinet. The Mongol emperors had no recorded military education as such, nor did Hannibal. It is recalled that most of the military leaders of the Continental Army had no formal military schooling and little military training, learning their military trade on the field of battle.

General Forrest also gained his military education in the contest of arms, but otherwise was illiterate in common "book-learning." General Wolseley, commander in chief of the British Army, wrote of Forrest:

... He had no knowledge of military science nor of military history to teach him how he should act, what objective he should aim at, and what plans he should make to secure it. He was entirely ignorant of what other generals in previous wars had done under very similar circumstances. What he lacked in book lore he was to a large extent compensated for by soundness of his judgment upon all occasions and by his power of thinking and reasoning with a great rapidity under fire, and under all circumstances of surrounding peril or of great mental or bodily fatigue. Panic found no resting-place in that calm brain of his, and no danger, no risk, cowed that dauntless spirit. Inspired with true military instincts, he was verily nature's soldier. It would be difficult in all history to find a more varied career than his, a man who, from the greatest poverty, without any learning, and by sheer force of character alone, became the great fighting leader of fighting men, a man in whom an extraordinary military instinct and sound common sense supplied to a very large extent his unfortunate want of military education. His military career teaches us that the genius which makes men great soldiers is not to be measured by any competitive examination in the science or art of war. In war, Napoleon said, men are nothing; a man is everything. It would be difficult to find a stronger corroboration of this maxim than is to be found in the history of General Forrest's operations.[3]

When one examines the roster of the world's successful guerrilla leaders, the lack of traditional military education and military professionalism, when compared with accomplishment, becomes both impressive and baffling. For example, Charles W. Thayer in his book *Guerrilla* makes the

point that during World War II, "Mikhailovitch," the mythical leader of the Chetniks, who gave Hitler's legions such a
bad time in the mountains of Yugoslavia, "was a professional
soldier who knew all about the potentialities of guerrilla warfare and how it is conducted."[4] Tito, on the other hand, a
contemporary and leader of another Yugoslav faction, ". . . was
a professional revolutionary agitator — rather than a professional soldier — who knew next to nothing about military
matters or guerrilla warfare when he took to the hills."[5] Moreover, Mikhailovitch had not only a staff of competent professional officers but most of the weapons of the defeated Royal
Yugoslav Army, which were not captured by the Germans in
the initial invasion. To begin with, Tito had neither, though
subsequently he recruited a number of professional staff
officers.

Thayer continues:

The paradox is more apparent than real. Looking over the list
of successful modern guerrilla leaders, we find practically none
who had previous military experience. Mao Tse-Tung was a student and librarian and subsequently a professional trained revolutionary. Ho Chi Minh was a socialist agitator and his chief
lieutenant, Giap, was a French-trained teacher of history. Castro
was a lawyer. Ben Bella and Belkacim Krin were non-commission-
ed officers during the war who turned to politics as soon as they
were discharged. The only partially successful guerrilla with professional military training was George Grivas of Cyprus whose
movement was devoted practically exclusively to terrorism and
was modeled not on what he learned in military schools but on
his study of communist methods . . . In the Indo-China War, four
senior French generals including a marshal were defeated in the
end by the history teacher Giap. Probably the most successful
counter-insurgent leader, as we have noted, was Magsaysay, an
auto mechanic turned guerrilla, turned politician.[6]

Garibaldi was not a great general in the consensus of most military experts, but he was an unparalleled guerrilla fighter who improvised decisive moves on the spur of the moment. He won memorable victories over incredible odds.

It would appear, if it is indeed not completely accurate, that since the guerrilla is usually an outcast from his particular society and is a have-not who opposes a particular government, he normally would not enter the educational stream provided to the military of that country. His entry into military activities is often as an outsider, but apparently this denial of military education has not hampered guerrilla leaders from becoming formidable military opponents. Thayer offers this explanation:

The unorthodoxy of guerrilla operations is an obstacle for a professional soldier in whom orthodox methods have been inculcated during his entire career. However, as Prussian-trained Lettow-Vorbeck demonstrated, this is not insurmountable provided the officer has the initiative and intelligence to forget his military school sand-table exercises. Experience would thus seem to suggest that skills in orthodox military tactics and strategy are not an essential qualification for a guerrilla commander. On the contrary, they would appear to be a liability.[7]

As far as background and military professionalism are concerned, the foregoing shows conclusively that an absence of military education or previous military indoctrination does not seem to hamper a guerrilla leader from crushing his opponents, who are usually better educated and trained militarily. Neither does it seem to work to the detriment of other military leaders who have ascended to the topmost ranks in history, as a few examples have also shown. The experiences of these insurgent forces under their unusual leaders alone should serve as a great impetus to giving second thoughts to conventional military training. Furthermore, they strongly support the concepts of creativity in warfare previously discussed.

We must not be misled into thinking that high intellectual ability or prolonged education alone are sufficient to provide the media through which the mind is stimulated to a greater creative activity, or to an enrichment of the creative product. Military training and schooling themselves do not stimulate creativity. They extend and deepen knowledge. They can extend the techniques the artist may utilize as an artisan in the application of the idea to the canvas or the total information within which the subconscious nurtures a creative thought. They can produce superior artisans or technicians, but they, alone, can never produce artists.

The bitter experience of France in 1940 emphatically shows that the value of a military education in itself or of a high intelligence quotient as a determinant in rendering men military geniuses is extremely doubtful. Few of Napoleon's generals were broadly educated in formal schools. Napoleon, in 1808, at the zenith of his power, founded the famous military school of St. Cyr. After the Napoleonic wars, Jomini and a host of other French generals sponsored intensified programs of schooling for future generals of France. Since then, despite added emphasis on schooling, France has suffered repeated catastrophic defeats.

The long held view that superb physical prowess is necessary for leadership is an absurdity. Whereas Alexander, Caesar, and Patton were superb athletes as well as outstanding leaders, Napoleon Bonaparte could hardly be considered as a member of that elite muscular coterie. Marshal de Saxe achieved some of his greatest victories while carried on a stretcher.

On the other side of the ledger, there are some uniformities of character or situation that give clues to creativity or stimulate it. What are they? First, nonconformity, which seems to be characteristic of creative persons, also prevails among recognized capable military leaders. Many have displayed independence, irascibility, and eccentricity. Alexander the Great exercised his authority without restraint. Some of the Mongolian chieftains appeared uncontrollable in their sadistic impulses. Napoleon, even before he became Emperor, dared to flout the authority of the Paris Commune many times. The stories of General Patton's irascibility are legend.

Most of the leaders, either because they were born that way or possibly as a result of circumstances in which they were elevated to positions depriving them of close contact with fellow soldiers of lower rank, appear to be persons who to a great extent can be described as loners. Most had remote, austere personalities.

Their kind see life in different terms from the normal; the battlefield to them is a grand canvas on which they paint in men and matériel. In a sense many of them, by virtue of their nonconformity, have freed themselves from tradition or from the normal pattern of military experience. Education is apparently, and here I speak of education in the stylized sense of formal nonmilitary schooling plus formal military schooling, not an essential feature to their success. Rather, what seems to be more important is experience — and this includes not only the experience of the battlefield or of life in general, but of that total experience which is the funneling of all types of knowledge into the intellect from whatever source. Many, like Napoleon and Patton, gained it by reading extensively. Creative military leaders have the ability to use this total experience better than the average officer. Regardless of the conforming pressures of military life, the creative leaders somehow have been able to maintain a separate identity; they have remained independent intellectually and, also, in a physical sense they work in a self-generated free environment.

Next, in a physical, or geographical, sense environment plays a major role in the quantity of creativity which these leaders have produced. This deserves amplification. The environment most conducive to creativity is one in which these individuals enjoyed freedom to use their creative intellect to manipulate the total resources at their disposal. These resources include, but are not limited to, the intellects of their staff, their troops, their administrative machinery for governing local populations to successfully support their military efforts, their weapons and other supplies, the intelligence on the enemy, the weather, and the terrain.

War provides the commander with an ideal creative environment. This is particularly true in an environment where a breakthrough of the enemy lines has taken place. Having left the restrictive laws and traditions of his homeland, the creative leader now feels psychologically free to operate in what is for him a free environment. It is in this type of an environment that Rommel thrived in North Africa. It was in that same theater and in a similar breakthrough environment that Montgomery, in his turn, did so well in his stab into the heart of German-held North Africa and his march into Tunisia. Patton found a similar situation and exploited it when his army was the southern flank of the American troops in France.

The benefit of the free environment also helps to explain some of the enormous successes enjoyed by the Mongols, for example, when they broke out into what was for them truly a new world, or by Alexander the Great when he finally broke through Persian resistance. From that time on, Alexander had practically unknown territories ahead of him.

Circumstances challenged his intellectual capacity to produce solutions to unknown problems, to enemies whose strength and character he did not know well, and to unknown lands which confronted him. Hannibal in his day operated in a completely free environment. As with Alexander, Hannibal operated away from the law, away from control of his own home government, and, except for those pressures which may have been exerted upon him by his allies or by the limitations of terrain or his own forces, he maneuvered and operated in optimum freedom.

Napoleon had the same advantages. This fact explains better than anything else some of the conditions and reasons for Napoleon's ability to operate with such complete success in his early years. He broke into Europe on the flood tide of revolutionary thought and action. Himself a man of boundless imagination, he remained relatively unhampered by supervision; operating in alien territory, he directed his early campaigns without consulting anyone. He was insistent that he alone be the master of his actions.

Napoleon's later strength may be attributed to the fact that his creativity extended not only into the military realm but into the political and international relations arena as well. He drew up a political organization in Europe and many laws that carried forth his personality and will, maintaining him in power even beyond the time that his military strength had begun to wane. After some fifteen years of dazzling and innovative performance, Napoleon had exhausted his creative energies. He was becoming a prisoner of his own patterns, and his enemies, more numerous and more skilled, had begun to anticipate his tactics. It has been said that when the French Emperor had 35,000 troops, he was far more creative than with vast legions.

However, undoubtedly one of the vital reasons for his

decline, surmised by historians, is the fact that his creativity seemed to wane. He suffered the dilemma of many artists, only his was of greater magnitude. With many artists, their creative zest in one field may become exhausted but, if they are versatile and energetic enough and time is in their favor, they are able to enter into new fields to devise new art modes, forms, or methods. Napoleon's art form was the battle, his arena the continent of Europe. So far as the resources of the Continent were concerned, he had manipulated and used them many times and in many forms, exhausting his creative talent. His ideas had no place for further expression within the confines of continental Europe. England had denied him the sea. Russia had denied him Asia, and a weakening flesh had drained him of time. His creative spirits atrophied and he fell.

The tragedy of war for the professional soldier is that it must end. Most capable military men have only begun to realize their intellectual talents before they are killed in battle or the end of war throttles their full expression. War permits the soldier in the philosophical and psychological senses to realize himself. It provides a release of the unconscious — of the id, as psychologists have described it. War not only releases the creative talents of selected leaders and individuals who are able to use them in their ideal role, but it also is a release mechanism for these talents on a much broader scale. War releases the talents of whole civilizations. E. P. Potter and Admiral Chester W. Nimitz say in *Sea Power:*

The history of Greece in the century following Salamis demonstrates that war, when not too destructive, can be a stimulating and civilizing influence. For warfare, along with its undoubted evils, shatters the restrictions of entrenched custom and tradition and compels nations to reassess their ideas and institutions. It gives a victor a sense of accomplishment and a new confidence in his own powers. Certainly no people in history have been electrified into greater creative activity than the Greeks were after their triumph over Persia. As others do, out of the ruins left by the war, the Athenians erected a new and greater Athens, a city of surpassing grandure, whose magnificent ruins excite the imaginations of men to this day.[8]

CHAPTER TEN

The Creativity of the Guerrilla

People's armed forces beginning only with primitive
. . . rifles and hand grenades have in the end defeated
the imperialist forces armed with modern planes,
tanks, heavy artillery and atom bombs. Guerrilla forces
have ultimately defeated regular armies. "Amateurs"
. . . never trained at any military school have eventually defeated professionals graduated from military
academies.

LIN PIAO's *Manifesto*

BAFFLING AND ANNOYING to a growing number of established
governments — long more disdained than respected by
straight-laced military professionals — the wily guerrilla has
finally brashly shouldered his way into respectable military
society. No longer can he be snubbed as an inconsequential
interloper, for he has become a formidable battlefield con-
tender. Moreover, to the deep embarrassment of our great
nation, he no longer is comfortably another country's enigma,
but instead has become ours to solve, and *solve it we must!*
We must reconnoiter every avenue to find the answer to this

enigma, and we must not equivocate over this onerous task.

I am firmly convinced that the discovery of the antidote to the growing guerrilla infestation hinges on whether our political and military leaders gain a proper understanding of some fundamental military philosophy that so far has evaded their discerning minds and those of the throng of sophisticated research organizations in which our leaders have entrusted the job of finding solutions. Very simply, this philosophy forms the nucleus from which have evolved the disturbing new ideas telling how a military inferior can manage the defeat of a superior, but conventional, antagonist. The philosophy was first formulated and advanced by T. E. Lawrence, better known as "Lawrence of Arabia" and author of *The Seven Pillars of Wisdom.* For more than twenty-five years he has been discreetly plagiarized by Red China's boss, Mao Tse-tung, and his cohorts. They have refined and sorted Lawrence's philosophy into manageable principles for battlefield practitioners who, in turn, are unleashing it in an unnerving, international program of guerrilla warfare.

Erudite military analysts customarily interpret the guerrilla phenomenon as a belligerent outburst by dissidents lashing at social, political, and economic injustice. Moreover, the analysts take the viewpoint that the guerrilla's vehemence toward the system and the authorities that represent the system stimulates him to fight against what would otherwise be insuperable military odds. However, in my opinion, our scholarly studies of the phenomenon too often mistakenly focus on the day-to-day outcroppings of guerrilla ire, such as bold sallies against government outposts, or the seemingly senseless assassination of an official, or the clever evasion of a well planned attack by government forces, rather than getting at the root ideas that nourish these exasperating deeds. I truly believe that, with the exception of only one man, little or nothing has been done by any individual in the West to uncover the prevailing philosophy from which these ideas germinate. This individual, the noted British historian and military analyst, Captain B. H. Liddell Hart, interpreting Lawrence, had many years ago attempted to alert the West to the significance of a new, and hitherto undeveloped military philosophy. It portended vast upheavals in conventional thinking by showing the potential of Lawrence's guerrilla warfare philosophy.

Liddell Hart, like Mao Tse-tung, has divined the true meaning of what Lawrence tersely told the world. These astute observers recognized that the guerrilla phenomenon is fundamentally intellectual, with Lawrence as its apostle. It provides the framework for a military technique for cleverly and inexpensively forcing one's military will upon an opponent. Unfortunately, it has been subverted by the Communists. They are applying it practically at tactical and strategic levels and it has gained so much favor in their eyes that they now consider it the most powerful weapon in their military arsenal, and a much more subtle weapon than the atomic bomb. Mao, long ago growing aware of the potential of guerrilla warfare, which is underpinned by Lawrence's philosophy, prophesied ". . . the guerrilla campaigns being waged in China today are a page in history that has no precedent. Their influence will be confined not solely to China in her present anti-Japanese struggle, but will be worldwide."[1] His forecast, made in 1937, bears our nation bitter fruit today.

Ironically, Mao is exploiting an intuitive intellectual breakthrough spawned in Western culture, coming from the mind of Lawrence at a critical period when he was fighting Turks in Arabia. Western military leaders seem to have blatantly disregarded or have failed to comprehend what Lawrence tried to tell them, both when he was an active leader and later through his writings. These leaders respect him for his accomplishments, but seem to regard him not as a military genius so much as an eccentric who won a war through sheer good luck.

Because they are philosophically inclined, the Chinese have understood Lawrence and, wisely, have not treated him either so casually or as an oddity. However, I consider the Chinese out-and-out plagiarizers and flatly disagree with most scholars of Chinese military history who would argue that guerrilla warfare is merely a sophisticated extension of the ancient maxims taken from General Sun Tzu's teachings on the art of war. These grossly regurgitated, monotonous sayings come up in many forms, inane and awkwardly tailored to tactical events to prove a controversial point.

Hard evidence shows the Chinese Communists' respect for Lawrence. His ideas were first exposed when the *Oxford Times* printed eight copies of *The Seven Pillars of Wisdom*. Four years later a subscriber's edition appeared and became a best seller overnight, although difficult to buy because of its limited printing. Some copies are certain to have made their way early into Chinese hands, and their contents were soon digested by inquisitive oriental minds, for we learn from Haldore Hanson in his book, *Humane Endeavour,* written shortly thereafter, that in about 1936 General Lu Chang Ts'oa, commander of the Central Hopei Communist guerrillas, had a Chinese translation of *The Seven Pillars* at his elbow when Hanson visited the general's field headquarters. The general was candid enough to admit the startling information that he and other guerrilla commanders considered *The Seven Pillars* "one of the standard reference books on strategy,"[2] which is a viewpoint United States military leadership does not share, as far as I am aware. Some authorities go so far as to claim Mao extracted the heart of the book and published it as a manual on guerrilla tactics to be used in the instruction of future guerrilla leaders.

Obscured in Chapter 33 of *The Seven Pillars* lie the secrets that, when put into practice, won a war. The chapter is definitely "off beat," abstruse to say the least; it departs from the easy style of the rest of the book, and almost seems to have been inserted as an afterthought.

After a few preliminary battles, Lawrence found himself in a tight position. Strapped for men and guns to fight the traditional, Western-style, mass-murder war, his task of defeating the Turks conventionally loomed well-nigh insurmountable. Racking his brain for solutions, he pondered the standard military classics of Clausewitz, Moltke, Foch, and others. He also reflected on Napoleonic methods, from all of which teachings have been passed on to Western military leaders and have become the foundation of Western military systems to this day. Considering war in the abstract, he found that these works made little sense. Furthermore, he had neither the troops nor other resources for waging the kinds of war they proposed. As a result, he rejected their extermination philosophies with disdain, bluntly asserting, "They disgusted me with soldiers [meaning, of course, the Prussianistic, tradition-oriented ones], wearied me of their officious glory, making me critical of all their light."[3] It is quite apparent now, however, that guerrillas have wholeheartedly accepted and sustained what is to us a peculiar brand of Lawrencian logic. Peculiar or not, it seems to have worked many times for them.

As he continued to mull over how he would fight his own private war, Lawrence found distasteful another idea the sages advocated — that victory must be purchased by blood, blood that has been shed to destroy the enemy only through one grinding process, the brutal slugging match called modern mass battle. He did not want to fight battles as we know them. His mind under duress performed intuitively and produced an ingenious idea that he expressed abstractly, as became the style of the critical chapter. Traditional armies had to have some objective to capture, he reasoned — "a hill, a town, or a line of trenches." What, if instead, he would give them "no aim" or in other words, no objective? What if he would not stand up to his enemy and slug it out toe to toe in battle? What if he would not dig trench systems or build rocky desert forts?

He was in an ideal position to follow this line of logic since his Arabs were not organized into recognizable military formations, and, coupled with this, they had horses and camels to give them admirable mobility in a vast desert, which would make them "like vapor to shoot at." The Turks, he reasoned, could sit where they were or where they wanted, welcome to the tiny part of Arabia their warm bodies actually held, but the rest of Arabia was completely open, beckoning to be used as Lawrence and his chieftains wanted, his forces being, as he conceived, ". . . an idea, a thing intangible, invulnerable, without front or back, drifting about like a gas."[4] This guerrilla-formented tricky strategy is curiously like the kind we find evolving under the Viet Cong in Viet Nam today.

Lawrence extended this line of thinking through to a conclusion that had none of the flavor of "unconditional surrender," none of the harsh dogma requiring the destruction of the will to resist through the powerful leverage of military force exterted in great battles. Instead, he conceived of avoiding titanic battles entirely so as to wear down the enemy morale, with the idea, as Lawrence says, that the enemy ". . . would go [away] quietly" and "the war would end."[5] This is Mao's "protracted war" in a nutshell. Like Lawrence's, it postpones the decisive battle until the balance of power is in favor of the guerrilla forces, and the enemy has no choice but annihilation or escape, an obvious parallel to the potential situation in Viet Nam.

Lawrence had irrevocably broken with traditional methods of fighting a war. He had "thrown away the books." He started this new kind of war, his mind uncluttered, unbiased, free, and ready to create from original materials, battle-winning combinations. As he stated, "We kindergarten soldiers were beginning our art of war in the atmosphere of the Twentieth Century, receiving our weapons without prejudice."[6] Weapons, to Lawrence, had a much broader meaning than just guns or swords. To him, the term meant every device, every man, every bit of land, and the variety of life and geography that land supported, including, of course, the cities, the peoples, and then, finally, the guns and swords and materials of war he might lay his hands on. These, he gave to his mind to manipulate creatively into new tactics and clever artifices for the battlefield, if and when he had to grapple with the Turks. He had no qualms if meet the enemy he must, since he considered them stupidly conventional, an enemy who thought the Arabs would fight according to gentlemanly, "Marquess of Queensbury" rules, or if necessary, "slug it out," according to the "book."

Lawrence was now faced with the task of filling the vacuum the rejection of conventional tactics had left. He saw the solution in man himself, in man's magnificent ability to change his environment so as to improve his situation on this earth. He saw this ability emanating from man's greatest asset and most powerful instrument, the brain. In Lawrence's thinking, the mind was the prime mover in war, and the ultimate determiner of victory. He had enough of books; he no longer looked for pat formulas to liquidate a particular military problem; rather he pressured his mind to solve the problem innovatively. When he subsequently concluded, "Our kingdom lay in each man's mind,"[7] he unknowingly set the stage for political and military thinking on the fighting of war, widely divergent from the time-honored methods, that have since unleashed new, dynamic and uncontrollable forces in war that have basically altered the character of war forever.

Both Lawrence and Admiral Mahan speak of a special quality or operative character of the mind that makes artists. This is its intuitive and creative faculty. Of the guerrilla's ingenuity we are painfully aware. It is, in fact, the earmark of a guerrilla — his distinguishing characteristic. Guerrillas are known to rely on imaginative leadership, distraction, surprise, and mobility. Creative, innovative minds fashion ambushes, unorthodox tactics and clever ways of killing, lining pits with poisoned bamboo spikes to impale the unwary, fashioning zip guns and lead-pipe explosives, and a host of fiendish devices. The guerrilla's mind is transformed into a lethal substance.

Lawrence was fully aware that all individuals are potentially creative, and an individual's creativity waits only to be tapped when the time and circumstances are appropriate. He had concluded that the really brilliant victories in warfare had been created by intuitive leaders. He felt the line for expected intuition need not be drawn at the leaders, but could include all men if they were given the chance to use it. Consequently, he literally discharged the men from the ranks and made them all individuals and independent military operators, saying, "Governments saw men only in mass; but our men, being irregulars, were not formations, but individuals."[8]

Mao shares Lawrence's viewpoint and has stated that even

in the most ignominious of the peasants, great creative talent lies latent, needing only to be properly motivated and activated in order to lead them to pinnacles of achievement.

Lawrence and his men needed much less than the average soldier in weapons and traditional objectives for they gained far more than the traditional soldier in the materials the mind could manipulate. He differentiated and separated the individual soldier from the mass battle formation. He returned the soldier to himself, making him again reliant upon his own creative talents, a free agent — separated from the structures of rigid military formations, an "intangible" force at liberty to maneuver where it chose. The intellect was free and supreme. Lawrence had finally developed for mankind a philosophical military doctrine for a force that had humbled even Napoleon.

Incredibly, the elements of this philosophy, in spite of their military flavor, are the same stimuli that furnish the life-giving drive to artists, the creatively talented who reach pinnacles of success in other fields of man's endeavor. Lawrence was an eminent military artist, as is true of the lesser guerrillas, who may be less talented but are nonetheless serious artists in their own right.

The same creative stimuli and now-accepted creative processes play equal roles and follow similar creative courses in the development of the ideas of all creative people, be they painters or the disinherited guerrilla. Only now the guerrilla is tougher than ever before, because shrewd battle practitioners, like Mao and Ho Chi Minh, have honed the philosophy razor-sharp, giving it an unprecedented, bloody lethality. It is foolhardy, not only for the military leaders, but for the political leaders of this nation, to gloss over the meaning of Lawrence and the obvious relationship that creativity bears to Lawrence's military philosophy. True, no one wants to face the upsetting facts that must be faced if we are in any way to acknowledge that Lawrence and the human behaviorists are right. It means that we must spend long hours trying to *think* through their meaning. It means that some highly placed, powerful forces are going to have to do a lot of about-facing; it means they too will then have to fly in the face of strong traditions to make changes in schools, doctrine, and thought.

Human behaviorists generally agree that an individual's creative intellectual faculty accelerates as a greater sense of freedom from restriction grows. The guerrilla is fortunately endowed with two forms of freedom; one is intellectual, and the other physical. The first he achieves when he sheds or escapes from the restrictive mantle of law and order imposed by his former government. This law and order are the mark of a firmly established society or government. Law, order, and custom tell a man what he can or cannot do within the framework of a government or society.

A soldier is saddled with an extra measure of restriction when he must observe the additional military regulations, codes of conduct, and tactical doctrines essential to the operation of a disciplined and effective modern fighting force. Civilian and soldier alike feel this ominous pressure on their natural impulses and any creative ideas that stem from these impulses or the need to solve a particular problem innovatively. Unfortunately, most men find it too difficult to try to think innovatively under these burdens; they lose hope, their intellectual energy wanes, and they sink into apathy, content to follow the channels of thought approved by the omnipotent majority.

However, in sharp contrast, virtually no law hampers a guerrilla. This often achieves for him the second freedom — the freedom of physical movement which leads him into new avenues of experience and adventure and adds to his total reservoir of knowledge.

A local civilian can assist a guerrilla in two ways that help to put teeth into the creative idea. First, the civilian can be a sympathetic supporter to the extent that he can wield a weapon, contribute food, and help the guerrilla sabotage the enemy mission. These potentially helpful elements to the guerrilla cause are in the subconscious of the guerrilla and are available to be used in conjunction with other facts for developing an idea for solving a tactical problem. He uses the population as one of his art materials with all others at the disposal of his intellect.

There is, however, an even more critical role the local population plays, and that role is the receptive audience. A creative artist, such as a painter who has done a colorful landscape, must have an audience, or his creative idea developed in the painting means relatively nothing to him except the pleasure it may have given him to paint it. In order for his painting to sell, an audience has to be available and members within the audience must like the idea enough to buy it, support it, or die for it. In the same way the guerrilla must communicate his ideas to the populace. Part of these ideas may be in the form of ideological propaganada to condition the population for further exploitation of it by the guerrilla. Because of the importance of communication in the realization of the ideas of an artist, it becomes important for anti-guerrilla forces to cut the guerrilla's communication with the people of the countryside.

As described earlier, highly creative people are well known nonconformists. They are people in whom the spirit of rebellion frequently surges. They are also known as divergent thinkers — in other words, they simply don't go along with the crowd. One well-known psychiatrist goes so far as to describe a creative person (almost as if he were describing the Viet Cong) as primitive and more cultured, more destructive and more constructive, and crazier and saner than the average person. He is a type who almost always unconsciously resents many of the pressures of the society that attempt to make him conform. Certainly, when we reflect on the nature of the guerrilla, particularly his usual vendetta against the established government, plus his oddities in and outside of combat, we see the close resemblance his characteristics have to those we consistently find in the artist. The guerrilla, unfortunately, is creative in a destructive sense, destructive to established standards of life and culture and material things associated therewith. His ideas find expression in the creation of a devilish ambush, in sly attacks on our airfields, and in wanton attacks on hamlets, whereas other recognized artists of fame in other fields of man's endeavors channel their creativity into constructive monuments and into immortal paintings. Regardless of the wide disparity between the two activities, they both originate from powerful creative insights and drives.

Motivation is another of the characteristics prevalent in creative people and a factor that makes the guerrilla operate so effectively. As one authority, Dr. T. W. Adams, remarks in *Army Research and Development News*, "All types of people are potentially creative when they are working with intense motivation and self-discipline in the right environment."[9] Michael Drury suggests:

It is false to imagine that creativity just happens. The capacity to be creative is inherent in human beings, but the utilization of that capacity is hard work. It is not hobbies or "taking of courses" or "keeping busy." Creativity is work that goes some place: *it is sustained effort toward an ideal* [Author's italics].[10]

One of the earmarks of a guerrilla is his high political motivation, and it is this motivation which drives him on in his tactical tasks and helps him to innovate.

Motivation also helps him verify an idea by seeing it through to its conclusion.

The guerrilla is like any artist in this respect. A good artist will have an idea that he commits to the canvas or uses to shape pliant clays into a fine vase or human form, but it may take years for him to produce it. But because he is emotionally involved and dedicated to his idea and its realization, he will not be easily dissuaded from his absorbing task. The same involvement and dedication grip the guerrilla. Time is not a factor of major concern. In his viewpoint, Mao echoes Lawrence's indifference to the time needed to attain victory, preferring to call it "protracted conflict."

A guerrilla is habitually a ragtag renegade, hunted, frequently forced to go it alone, fortunate if accompanied by a few comrades. In the compelling struggle for self-preservation, his intellect begins to effervesce and turn out more and shrewder ideas. They germinate rapidly because circumstances are so favorable. He has freedom from the constriction of censure of his fellowmen. He is a nonconformist, with strong motivations. From the natural resources in the land about him, from the weapons, ammunition, and other supplies he has captured, using the local populace to his advantage, initiative and intuition force his intellect to innovation and invention.

Lawrence deftly manipulated these boundless resources not usually tapped in any similar manner by traditional armies. He made a pointed reference to how he would do this. His strength in men but marginal, as he said:

It seemed the [total] assets in this element of the war were ours. If we realized our raw materials and were apt with them, then climate, railway, desert, and technical weapons could also be attached to our interests.[11]

We see the fruits of this philosophy ripening today all too clearly in too many places of the world. It is a philosophy that allows guerrillas wide latitudes in action and in creating their own tactics and strategy of a local brand conditioned entirely to their resources, their environment, and the needs of the moment. They are like artists experimenting and creating with paint and brush, using the jungles, the mountains, and the captured supplies to create weapons and war. The creative artist within the guerrillas makes them the grim military problem they are to their enemies. Navy Commander Donald R. Morris points out precisely this artistic and creative quality of guerrillas in his *Washing of the Spears,* describing the character of Shaka, leader of the Zulu nation, who badly mauled the British.

Shaka was a charismatic leader with a skeptical and inquiring mind. He was a military genius who developed a new weapon which was a shortened heavier kind of spear or assegai and innovative tactics for devastating in-fighting. He saw each battle not as a set piece bounded by tradition but as a challenge to his ingenuity in developing new strategies that used surprises, deception, terrain and rapid movement in his advantage.

What Mao Tse-tung plagiarized so profitably from Lawrence has been fashioned recently into an elaborate program for world conquest, Lin Piao's *Manifesto.*

Using our insight into creativity, it is possible to see why Lin Piao's *Manifesto* makes sense to his way of thinking as well as giving it meaning and substance to naïve Western politicians and generals. The conclusions may appear to be improbable, but they offer the only rational explanation

for Lin Piao going so far out on a limb. The accomplishments of guerrilla warfare to date prove it is workable, at
least on a limited scale. Mao Tse-tung's reliance on the
peasant, his avowed belief in their creative talents, plus some
of his gleanings from T. E. Lawrence, give credence to the
theory evolved in the *Manifesto.*

Lawrence spoke of the protracted war. So does Piao.
Lawrence fostered the rising of the people against the
foreigner. Piao says, "It has become an urgent necessity for
the people in many countries to master and use people's wars
as a weapon against U.S. imperialism. . . ."[12] Lawrence, from
the vastness of the desert, appeared and struck Turkish
strongholds in the cities. Piao says, "Mao . . . during the War
of Resistance against Japan developed his thought on the
establishment of rural base areas and the use of the countryside to encircle the cities. . . ."[13] Furthermore, "Mao's theory
. . . is of outstanding and universal practical importance for
the present revolutionary struggles of all oppressed peoples
and nations."[14]

Piao has placed his confidence in the peasantry for good
reasons. The peasant farmer, on the whole, is a hardy speci-
men. He is accustomed to the outdoors, he can work alone
with meager tools and simple food. He does not reside in
a constricted environment and is less hampered by the law,
especially in some areas of the world. The foregoing characteristics may be recognized as elements found to stimulate
creativity.

Mao also employs human resources in urban areas, where
he considers people of the intellectual caliber suited to
implement his political objectives via the military product
of urban society. As Piao quotes Engels, "The Emancipa-
tion of the proletariat . . . will have its specific expression
in military affairs and create the specific new method."[15]

I would add, further, the new mentality—giving individual men and leaders on the battlefield greater latitude for creative expression, in the style of Lawrence.

Mao Tse-tung has provided a masterly summary of the strategy and tactics of peoples' wars:

You fight in your way and we fight in ours; we fight when we can win and move away when we can't.

In other words, you rely on modern weapons and we rely on highly conscious revolutionary people; you give full play to your superiority, and we give full play to ours; you have your way of fighting, and we have ours. When you want to fight us, we don't let you and you can't find us. But when we want to fight you, we make sure that you can't get away and we hit you squarely . . . and wipe you out. When we are able to wipe you out, we do so with a vengeance; when we can't, we see to it that you do not wipe us out.[16]

In the Chinese Civil War, Mao enumerated the basic tactics of guerrilla warfare as follows:

The enemy advances, we retreat; the enemy camps, we harass; the enemy tires, we attack; the enemy retreats, we pursue.

Guerrilla war tactics were further developed during the War of Resistance against Japan. In the base areas behind the enemy lines everybody joined—civilian population, men and women, old and young. . . . Various ingenious methods of fighting were devised, including sparrow warfare, land mine warfare, tunnel warfare, sabotage warfare, and guerrilla warfare on lakes and rivers.[17]

A footnote in Lin Piao's article defines sparrow warfare:

. . . a popular method of fighting created by the Communist-led anti-Japanese guerrilla and militia units behind the enemy lines. . . . It was used flexibly by guerrillas or militiamen, operating in threes or fives, appearing or disappearing unexpectedly (like sparrows) and wounding, killing . . . and wearing out the enemy forces.[18]

I have emphasized many times in my previously published work the hard fact that good fighters have not always been the most extensively trained, but rather the most ingenious in intellectual quality. A curiously parallel viewpoint is to be found in Piao's *Manifesto:*

Since Lenin led the Great October Revolution to victory, the experience of innumerable revolutionary people who rise up with only their bare hands at the outset finally succeeded in defeating the ruling classes, who are armed to the teeth. People's armed forces beginning only with primitive . . . rifles and hand grenades have in the end defeated the imperialist forces armed with modern planes, tanks, heavy artillery and atom bombs. Guerrilla forces have ultimately defeated regular armies. "Amateurs" . . . never trained at any military school have eventually defeated professional graduates from military academies. [19]

Whereas the guerrilla has heretofore erupted sporadically throughout the history of warfare, unnerving Napoleon in Spain, and the Greek government many years later, helping to topple Chiang Kai-shek, and overthrowing Batista, T. E. Lawrence was the first to give philosophical substance to his methods. What Mao has done via Lin Piao is to broaden the sphere of application for his philosophy to all urban areas of the world. He revealed its shadow but not its Lawrencian substance in the *Manifesto,* and is now prepared to implement it militarily to reach his political objective—world domination.

CHAPTER ELEVEN

Some Further
Thoughts on Creativity

Successful acts of war are not premeditated acts;
they are spontaneous, dictated by military intuition.
MOLTKE

THE LOGICAL OUTGROWTH of the viewpoint offered earlier
that "creativity may require the temporary suspension of
logic"[1] has led to experimentation with this objective in view.
Doctors Parloff and Handlon, after long study, found that
psychotherapy or drugs such as LSD and mescaline did aid
in suspending logic, thereby enabling a greater production
of creative ideas.

There have been other devices designed to help activate
idea production. Many of these, such as the Gordon, or
"Operational Creativity"[2] method, and the question technique are presented by Alex Osborn in *Applied Imagination*. There remains serious question as to whether these
methods tap subconscious resource levels. Nonetheless, they
offer some alternatives to those interested in researching
deeper into the creative processes or others who hope to
increase their own intellectual performance.

For a period after World War II, the military services

became enamored of "brainstorming." This involves the training of individuals or groups who are engaged in a joint problem-solving (brainstorming) effort to express freely all solutions that occur to them without attempting to evaluate either their own ideas or those of their fellow group members. The proponents of brainstorming have undertaken to demonstrate experimentally its usefulness in facilitating creative problem-solving.

The research evidence in favor of brainstorming is equivocal. The method may produce a lot of ideas, but a large number may lack quality, and the value of the remainder may be but marginal.

Whatever the merits of brainstorming are, the technique is geared to Pentagon committee deliberations, to the snugness and safety of the corporation conference chamber, and to the non-crisis professorial atmosphere of the typical scholarly research operation never confronted with a life-death, crisis decision. I doubt the practicality of the method for the regimental commander confronted with a problem in the heat of combat. Whom would he assemble for a brainstorming session? His battalion commanders, who are probably ten times more occupied than he? His staff, whom he'd have a hard time getting hold of if they were doing their jobs? Most likely he would not harass any of them in a nebulous search of their minds for an idea that should come from his. At any rate, a brainstorming group on the front line might encounter conflicting difficulty, drizzling ideas under a rain of shrapnel.

When Napoleon pointed out that "councils of war never fight" he got at the heart of the defect in the collective approach to solving combat problems. The case is well stated by philosopher William Ernest Hocking. He says of "corporate officialdoms":

[They] . . . are helpless and barren—the parties, bureaus, departments, cabinets, commissions—barren because of the inner cancellation of each other's certitudes. The composite program, prudentially polished, has every virtue in it but *life*. Where there is no personal vision, the people perish. . . . Could Hamlet have been written by a committee, or the Mona Lisa painted by a group of conferees? Could the New Testament have been composed as a conference report?[3]

The answer is emphatically "No!" Creative ideas do not spring from groups. They spring from individuals. The divine spark leaps from the finger of God to the finger of man. Finally, brainstorming does not meet realistically a possibly changed intellectual character of man, reduced as it is in combat to its primitive form, when it will function in accordance wth raw psychological patterns whatever the training may have been.

It is generally acknowledged that a creative person is dedicated to the problem-solving task. This means that his involvement with the task is, more or less, complete in both the mental and physical sense, but especially the former. Edison is a good example of an individual so involved. He spent intense periods of mental concentration on his inventions while living day and night in his laboratory. This period of involvement with the problem may not, during the period, produce the new idea, or the answer to a serious problem, but the answer starts to brew during the involvement and may come at an unexpected moment. One example, among countless that are now recorded, relates to André Marie Ampère (1775-1836), after whom the unit of electric current is named, a genius of childlike simplicity, who recorded in his diary the circumstance of his first mathematical discovery, according to Arthur Koestler's *The Act of Creation*.

On April 27, 1802, he tells us, I gave a shout of joy. . . . It was seven years ago I proposed to myself a problem which I have not been able to solve directly, but for which I had found by chance a solution, and knew that it was correct, without being able to prove it. The matter often returned to my mind and I had sought twenty times unsuccessfully for this solution. For some days I had carried the idea about with me continually. At last, *I do not know how*, I found it, together with a large number of curious and new considerations concerning the theory of probability. As I think there are very few mathematicians in France who could solve this problem in less time, I have no doubt that its publication in a pamphlet of twenty pages is a good method for obtaining a chair of mathematics in a college.[4]

Another great mathematician, Karl Friedrich Gauss, tells a friend how he finally proved a theorem on which he had worked unsuccessfully for four years.

At last two days ago I succeeded, not by dint of painful effort but so to speak by the grace of God. As a sudden flash of light, the enigma was solved. . . . For my part I am unable to name the nature of the thread which connected what I previously knew with that which made my success possible.[5]

A commander experiences similar varying degrees of dedication and an involvement. Greater dedication to military tasks is inevitable in wartime and becomes more so when he physically enters the combat area. His patriotism may motivate him, a sense of dedication to his mission may prevail, the stimulation of combat may be an inflaming factor, and the immediate challenge of contest with the enemy another. All may serve to intensify or heighten dedication to the combat, the problem-solving task.

A creative individual is aggressive for the goals he seeks. This aggressiveness may be expressed physically. Aggressiveness in an officer means courage, or courage plus other closely associated mental and physical attributes, which enable him to drive his men and himself through the terrifying phenomenon of combat and give him the will to continue despite all doubts and all cautious advice to the contrary. This was the character of Farragut at Vicksburg, of Hawke at Quiberon Bay, and MacArthur at Inchon. This courage is not unlike the courage demonstrated by Michelangelo, Whistler, Galileo, and a host of other artists who persevered with their ideas despite heartbreaking experiences and the lack of appreciation and acceptance by their contemporaries in art and the public.

Heroism in combat, such as the destruction of a machine-gun nest by a courageous soldier, is the perfect example of artistic accomplishment. In most cases, the elements for creativity existed. There was military knowledge in the trained soldier, motivation to stimulate aggressiveness, immersion in a situation, intense life or death involvement with a menacing machine gun, and frustration caused by the obstacle to the soldier's forward movement that had to be eliminated. Coupled with these elements, there is the freedom to take whatsoever measures are necessary without moral restraint.

The physical action a soldier takes under these circumstances is to observers precipitous, rash, or crazy in the extreme, but creatively viewed it is the explosion into action of a creative intellect who perceives more deeply than those around him, and at the risk of his life goes through with the task dictated by his mind and emotions. This thrust of the idea into action is much like that described by Henri Bergson, the noted French philosopher, discussing the relationship of the intuitional idea and its master.

Upon it depends all genuine insight into the mind and the living character of reality. Its transcendance of intellect will seem to some impossible, just as to swim seems impossible, save by first learning to hold ourselves up in the water. But just as in the latter instance one may break the vicious circle by leaping in and struggling, so in the former he may break the circle by frankly accepting the risk. Thus ". . . action will perhaps cut the knot that reasoning has tied."[6]

Danger forces the mind to innovate. In the case of the machine gun, it was a danger that had to be removed by a charge to the embankment, the tossing of a grenade, and the mop-up of the position. This done, the irritant is removed and the intellect subsides pending a new crisis.

The foreboding of death, or approaching death itself, may strongly impel a mind to creative ideation. Lasswell makes the point that if one were ". . . convinced that we would die tomorrow . . . our creativity today would undoubtedly be effected." Lasswell then proceeds to recount the case of the French mathematician Evariste Galois.

He allowed himself to be goaded into a duel with a political enemy in the turbulent year 1832, we have a spectacular instance of a threat that released the floodgates of creativity. All night before the duel, Galois, who was twenty years of age, wrote his last will and testament. As Bell (1937) put it, "What he wrote in those desperate last hours before the dawn will keep generations of mathematicians busy for hundreds of years." It may be doubted that as yet we have the tools that enable us to describe which predispositions, proportionate or disproportionate, will respond creatively to environmental challenges of great magnitude.[7]

Galois took a mortal wound on the dueling ground at dawn.

Frequently individual heroic deeds in combat cannot be rationally explained. We refer to a Medal of Honor winner as courageous, daring, or perhaps rash. However, little has been done in service research projects to search for motivations or ideas that developed to tell him that the act he would do was possible.

What explains his conviction that a deed was possible when it neither occurred to nor appeared to be so to a buddy in the same foxhole? Could it be that his deed showed that he too had the intuition that is found in men of unusual perception. The intuition that something needed to be done and could be done impelled him to go ahead and do it at great personal risk, even at the cost of life itself!

I am convinced that this is what happens since there is ample philosophical evidence that heroism is intuitional and is tied closely with strong emotional feelings, which a physical act — often a violent one — releases.

Recent research with animals seems to verify this. Biologists and psychologists have been prying into the stuff that makes a fight. In man, this stuff can be expressed destructively in war or murder, or, as these researchers feel, positively, as in the murals in the Sistine Chapel. The human impulses that make a fight, they say, are precisely those that make a masterpiece.

Undoubtedly there are military critics who will not question the fact that the great leaders discussed earlier were certainly creative, but they will argue that these leaders could be creative since they had the education and the resources in men and guns to be creative on the battlefield. But many of these people would find no place and no examples, nor recall any performances, of creativity among subordinate leaders or individual soldiers.

However, I am convinced, from what we have recently discovered about creativity, that many of the accomplishments of our junior battle leaders and the innovative deeds and inventions of individual soldiers to solve battlefield problems—to silence a thorny machine-gun nest or to rig up a special gadget for sighting a mortar, for example—were important innovative deeds derived initially from really very creative ideas.

General Omar Bradley cites an outstanding example of innovations of this type occurring when the Allied commanders, worried as to how they would break out of the hedgerows of Normandy, gained a tank sergeant's invention at the time of their greatest need. Twenty-nine-year-old Sergeant Curtis G. Culin from New York City fashioned a tusklike spade which he welded to a tank that permitted the tank to bore right through a hedgerow and open up an avenue for the following tanks and troops.

Within a week after he had demonstrated his idea to General Bradley, ordnance teams had equipped three out of every five tanks participating in the breakout with the device. The sergeant's idea is credited by many for giving the Americans the means they had long sought for the breakout and release of American power from the construction of the beachhead.

The quick thinking of a young forward artillery observer in one of General Patton's divisions vividly illustrates how one leader handled a dangerous situation creatively. His division commander recalls that a strong German patrol began to encircle and move in on the lieutenant's observation post, determined to wipe it out. In dire straits, unable to get help otherwise, the lieutenant quickly conceived an idea. He would bring down a whole battalion artillery concentration right on his own position!

He radioed the artillery to fire, then quickly he and his two enlisted men jumped down into the deep interior of their dugout, well protected from the hell that was now on its way. In moments the earth above exploded. When the fire lifted the lieutenant crawled into daylight and then gingerly searched around the area. The German patrol had vanished, disintegrated by the fire.

Now it never will be possible to determine precisely whether his idea to take this action was of either type "A" or type "B" creativity. However, something imaginative and daring had to be done. Action had to be swift. Consequently, I believe the lieutenant's idea came close to being of the dynamic type "B" intuitive creativity. Furthermore, he was like a real creative artist. He had vision to see that the patrol would be in the right place on the ground that his artillery could get at easily. He used the ground in another way—he crawled into it. He brought all his resources together within his mind first and then in action—using radio, the positions of his enemy, his dugout, and finally his battalion's guns all in a way to provide a really creative solution.

Another example is the case dramatically noted by S. L. A. Marshall in his record of the Normandy landing. He writes:

. . . of one bold man who, on his own initiative and wholly alone, simply moved ahead, kicked in the door of an "impregnable" enemy position, exterminated one enemy group after another, and totally changed the battle situation.[8]

That happens over and over again in combat.

To think that something like it does not happen on occasion in administration is to underestimate the importance of individual initiative at every level of activity. Such thinking also overestimates the powers of reason as opposed to emotional impulse and the fruits of professional training as they appear time and again in the mystic form of insight—whose reality the logician is reluctant to respect or even to recognize.[9]

Every soldier possesses resources his intellect can use or shape with clever implements or ideas which ultimately take form in deeds on the battlefield. Take, for example, the individual infantry rifleman: He has his M-16 rifle, also the trees, the weeds and other parts of ground around him, the dark of the night, fog, rain—or bright sunshine. He has the wealth of information on what to do in the face of the enemy that our Army school instruction has given to him. In a tight spot, if he gives his mind the task, it will create a way to outwit a dangerous enemy. His mind will quickly grasp an ingredient of the ground, a bush to hide behind, possibly a particularly good draw to use as cover to aid him; and his training will give him some information that will give him the best time to run forward, and whether to use bullet, grenade, or bayonet, or all three in what order. Whatever the arrangement, his mind will be used to manipulate creatively all the resources at the rifleman's disposal, including the physical, the coordinated sinew and strength of his body. Success and survival evolve from the mind in this way.

Ever since warrior kings relinquished their marshal's batons and left the direction of wars to their generals, emperors, kings, elected heads of nations, and dictators have been faced with the problem of selecting the correct captain to lead their nation's military forces. The job has not been easy, and gross error of judgment often fatal to a nation has resulted.

It is a recurring phenomenon of history that generals and admirals who begin a war are not necessarily those who win that war. President Lincoln had more than his share of McClellans. Lloyd George and Winston Churchill had their problems with finding war winners for the top assignments for His Majesty's forces. Brilliant peacetime performers have all too frequently proved disappointing and dismally inept in the throes of war.

This curious phenomenon occurs because those who are smooth enough to filter into the military hierarchy in peacetime are those who are best able to mold their thoughts and activities to the system, to understand it, and to use it to their advantage. To their peers and seniors, they are the ones who rock the boat the least. In a manner of speaking, their professional life, more likely than not, is merely a continuation of a role they have grown into and found convenient in their youth. If the truth were known, probably most were conforming children, who had a very orthodox youth. The step from local high schools and colleges into the military academies or directly into the services was not a difficult emotional step to negotiate, nor was the subsequent one into the service where conventions approximated their experiences.

These future wielders of power may be astute enough to realize the circumstances and clever enough to wield it to their benefit, but more likely they are the unwary, docile, and fortunate victims of the system and fall into the various echelons of the hierarchy as they are able to pace themselves in the current of organizational life. They find a better ability as they go through their careers to become a part of the deep-seated customs and traditions of the services, and in due time they filter to the top as both the models for and the perpetuators of the system, the supporters of its laws that will in turn perpetuate them and their way of life.

However, these circumstances, advantageous to them in peacetime, trip them in wartime. Then the fabric of tradition is ripped apart by a tremendous welter of new and completely unforeseen developments—Pearl Harbors, blitzkriegs, wolf-pack tactics, massive airborne assaults by gliders carrying men and weapons, plus transports dropping thousands of paratroopers. Vigorous political leaders stepping into the breach foment new ideas, new political and military organizations appear, and fantastic new weapons must be woven into the new fabric.

This is the occasion when those of the old system, suffering from indigestion of the intellect, unable to free themselves from the traditional patterns of thought and action, fall by the wayside, and their ranks are filled by those who have had little to do with structuring and perpetuating the prewar military doctrine, organization, and social patterns. Drastic alterations in traditional thinking are critically important to those who must cope with the mountainous wartime tasks, a type of thinking for which few peacetime wielders of power are prepared through peacetime military pursuits. Nor is total war a necessary requirement for such a situation to arise. Brush-fire wars or guerrilla warfare can be as disconcerting to professionals mired in peacetime military mentality as the challenge of a full-scale war.

It is the environment of the unknown, developed by war, that is thrust on the military leadership of a nation that causes opportunities to arise for their social and professional inferiors. Theirs has to this time been a frustrating lot— many of them nonconforming people who have found the peacetime military and social aspects of the military life incompatible with their personalities, many others unaware of the patterns of conformity the services demand for the price of recognition.

The characteristic described as nonconforming is often found in the creative person. While the presence of other characteristics, it has been noted, has varied among creative military men, it is of curious significance that some form of nonconformity has been evident in each, and at times this nonconformity has been the predominant recognizable trait.

Admiral Lockwood relates Sam Dealey's agony when he had to settle down to the none-too-pleasant life of a first-year man at the Naval Academy, where numerous restrictions imposed upon midshipmen and rigidly enforced by upperclassmen seriously disturbed him.

As a westerner, he had an inborn attitude of independence that rose in undisguised wrath whenever a senior midshipman took him for a ride because of some infraction of a rule so thin that Sam, often, could not even see it.[10]

Sam Dealey's first six months at the Naval Academy were filled with rebellion and his nights saturated with wrath. Partly because he had refused to buckle under as upperclassmen considered he should, he received so many demerits that they contributed to his having to leave the Academy after his first year. He later returned to graduate.

General MacArthur was a habitual nonconformist, both intellectually and in his personal dress—he frequently wore a flamboyant, nonregulation scarf, smoked a thin-stemmed corncob pipe, and sported a cap at a rakish nonregulation angle—things his subordinate commanders would certainly not have tolerated in their officers and men. George Patton is another example of a highly individualistic type. Patton's dress, like MacArthur's, was not regulation. He was unconventional in his behavior and his speech, so vituperously artful in invective that he was probably unsurpassed by anyone in any military service in the history of warfare. We can recall many similar traits in Alexander the Great, Lord Nelson, Napoleon, and many other leaders.

However, the vast majority of nonconformists are individuals who are less fortunate than the Alexanders, MacArthurs, and Pattons; consequently they suffer frustrations and, too frequently, are purposely subjugated, stepped on, reassigned, or set aside in some innocuous capacity because they are nonconformists and their ideas irritate authority and contradict the current thinking. While it is often difficult for them to succeed in the service, it is this type of person that holds promising credentials.

In recent studies conducted by the Department of Health, Education, and Welfare at the National Institutes of Health in Bethesda, Maryland, Dr. Parloff has found that headstrong children are geared to succeed. They are the type that will make creative contributions to the world "if," he relates, "someone does not knock their blocks off first."[11] In his study he determined that a top group that he tested rated "higher in ambition, independence, efficient use of their intelligence, perceptiveness, originality and rebelliousness."[12] These people had "a great sense of well-being, and they had little self-doubt."[13] While these characteristics pertained primarily to the group of young persons tested, in a subsequent test of creative adult scientists and a group of architects, Dr. Parloff found essentially similar qualities; "they too were generally dominant, headstrong, high in self-acceptance and persistence and low in socialization and willingness to conform and accept other standards."[14] These studies also found that among the creative men and boys "there was a skepticism, a wide range of interests, impatience with supervision, indifference to convention."[15] The parallel between the type of military leadership which has been discussed in this book so far, and that is highlighted in this particular paragraph, and the personalities and characteristics of Dr. Parloff's study is indeed striking!

Another characteristic of the creative type of person is that he has access to the stimulation from his unconscious. Obviously this has to do directly with his flexibility and his viewpoint on how he accepts the world about him and all the various rules, regulations, and laws which he must observe. It is possible to follow and to be disciplined by them, and yet to remain quite able to receive stimuli from the unconscious if one is willing to let one's mind function naturally, free from fear.

A creative person is also motivated by a desire to do the rigorous work required to test and modify his ideas and insights. Herein lies one of the most difficult tasks of the creative personality because it means that he has to pursue his ideas despite the great demands which will be made upon him intellectually and physically in carrying the ideas through to conclusion. Frequently, he will encounter listless to unreceptive supervisors or compatriots as he tries to sell his ideas. His enthusiasm will be jarred, his energies will be sapped, and unless he is an unusual individual who is able to shrug off or overcome these and many other obstacles set to deter him in his fulfillment, he will never realize his idea no matter how unique, valuable, or basically good it is. This is the experience of many artists; this is the curse of man toward man.

Many superiors will refuse to accept the idea though they see merit in it because it tends to upset their status; many will be jealous of new ideas; many, because the idea is not their own, will not accept it as feasible. Absurd? Not at all. This is a commonplace phenomenon. Many supervisors are trained to take something apart and tell what's wrong with it. At the present time, according to Dr. Harold F. Harding of Ohio State University, the emphasis of our educational system is on producing this type. Dr. Harding, himself a general, who is now retired in the U.S. Army Reserve says "generals and colonels tend to become critics and judges more than operators. It is only the rare colonel who tolerates, accepts, and encourages a climate of creativity."[16]

A few perceptive Pentagon officials are alarmed at the shortage of creativity in the armed services. Secretary of the Navy Paul Nitze claimed he would like to see "flexibility of mind, analytical thought processes, creativity, and imagination which will best qualify them [the commanders] to compete with the increasingly professional and intellectual civilian leadership."[17] But I wonder if part of the problem isn't the fault of the civilians themselves? At the Secretary level the military ideas may find an unreceptive attitude. The finger of guilt can be pointed at the civilian appointee, if indeed he is correct in his viewpoint. Just for him to wave a hand blithely and ask for more creativity is not going to generate more in his admirals or generals. He must tell them what he means by creativity, and how it is to be nurtured, and he must be its greatest stimulator by leadership example. Some basic schools on the subject should be started for all, and generals, admirals, and civilian political appointees should be required to attend sessions, and it would be a good idea if they were the first students.

The problem confronting a military man needing to do the rigorous work to test and modify his insights on the battlefield is great. It is a far greater burden to handle than the artist who may need only to put his idea on canvas, or his pen to paper, to convert his idea into architect's plans, or to see his invention through to a patent. The military creator has variable resources at his disposal. They may be as modest as a platoon of men and its weapons or a landing craft or a submarine or destroyer, or they may be a gigantic jigsaw that consists of regiments, many different large-caliber weapons, atomic bombs, and helicopter and air protection, or, as in the case of the Navy, the various flotillas on the sea, beneath the sea, and in the air.

While many of the other artists work with materials that enable them to express their ideas—the painter in oils to express his idea on the canvas; the architect with a pencil, pen, and T-square to illustrate his architectural plan— military creators must work largely in terms of people and their intellects. It is through these intellects that the total forces are wielded. Platoons just do not operate by themselves—they are led. Ships do not sail automatically— they are captained. But this by no means completely explains the problem either.

There is not only the monumental task of directing one's own troops toward the realization of the idea, but there is also the will and the material power of the opponent to be broken. Once joined in combat, the military leader must, more than any other creative type, have the will, the guts, the "stick-to-itiveness," the tenacity of purpose, despite all of the horror, heartbreak, and destruction which a sensitive man must bear, to achieve his idea and see it through. This is the type of tenacity well exemplified by German General Lothar Rendulic, who for five days stayed with his idea and ultimately withstood sustained attacks of Russian forces four times his number. He stood alone, with no help, no guidance, only the conviction of his ideas and the strength and tenacity to see them through to their ultimate conclusion.

Another element of the creative intellect is that the intellectual individual has a constantly growing knowledge about his field. The military intellect attains this awareness in various ways. Schools provide knowledge of new tactical ideas, new weapons systems, and methods of correlation and integration between tactics, weapons systems, and the uses of combined arms. Reading helps to amplify stored knowledge. A constant association with the profession in all its aspects also accomplishes this purpose. Observation and the experience of others falls into this category. Sam Dealey's favorite reading and writing while on combat submarine patrols in the Pacific were the patrol reports of other captains as well as his own. Experience, of course, is an important asset. All the prior study or the prior knowledge of any type does not compensate, and in no way compares with or prepares a man, entirely, for the experience of actual combat.

Ultimately, when creative insights begin to occur, they have a wealth of information upon which to draw from the unconscious. As with Nelson, officers and men who are adequately versed are entering upon a period of realization when they go to combat. As insights begin to develop, individuals feel a rebirth, and ideas begin tumbling out one after another. There is a period of discovery, not of new ideas, although this also pertains, but a discovery of man himself and his intellect, and the discoverer relishes the experience of successfully tried ideas and new thoughts. It is this sort of circumstance that I am certain many leaders have encountered in warfare, an experience substantiated by the performances of such leaders as Patton and Rommel, who gave free vent to their ideas in the physical realm.

CHAPTER TWELVE

Suggestions for the Battle Practitioner

But I do say that in many things we control [events] only up to a certain point. Beyond that point nebulous things which occur inside men's brains decide the issue.

REAR ADMIRAL DANIEL V. GALLERY

JOMINI WROTE ABOUT ART *and* mistakenly eulogized the military artisan instead of the artist in the process. Military men discuss military art with such naïveté that until now they have been largely unaware of the vital role that intuition and insight have played and will continue to play as long as man battles for the earth.

The military, with its talent for organization, with the promise that a broadened knowledge of creativity holds for success of men and leaders at the contest of arms, should bend to the task of leading this country in the accelerating national endeavor to harness creativity.

The maximum allowance of creative expression in the services can pay handsome dividends. Ideas can add to the more efficient function of an organization—they can spell tactical and strategic advantage for those organizations' commanders who have nurtured it. Men whose ideas are accepted will feel a higher sense of participation in the achievements of an organization of which they are members.

According to qualified authorities, the source of many of the frustrations, neuroses, and their frontline manifestation, combat fatigue, stems from a dissatisfaction developed by the suppression of normal intellectual expression. This suppression in the services results from a combination of rigid traditions, rules, and regulations—"the army way"—all of which overwhelm the inbred, much looser and freer, civilian way of doing things. If soldiers can be shown how to express themselves more creatively and can be led to feel a greater degree of freedom, morale will improve considerably, and the men will be more satisfied with their duty.

For the martinets and marginal believers who, in mixed emotions of fear and doubt, would cry, "But what about discipline?" I offer this advice. First, I would venture, there is no man who has ever commanded a fighting team of any size who has not found among his men working at the grim business of fighting, some who, in a pinch, have surprised him with a good suggestion. None of these subordinates has ever, because of his idea alone, jeopardized the success of a mission or caused a mutiny. Secondly, all ideas cannot be used, but a man who has one and finds a willing ear will feel a lot better if he has expressed it—gotten it off his chest, so to speak—even though it is impractical or inappropriate at the moment. Finally, what I am suggesting is that there be physical conformity for the good of the operations—that all pull the triggers—but there be mental freedom. The commander can demand the former by stimulating the latter.

There are some unique aspects of creativity that have special applications to the draftee as well as to the career enlisted man. They deserve serious thought.

In civilian life when an individual becomes dissatisfied with the conditions of his job, he can, on his own volition, quit his job and search for a new one that suits his personality or temperament. There are many advantages to this when it comes to allowing men to realize their full potential. Moreover, the benefits are particularly significant as far as creativity is concerned. To any individual, and more particularly to the creative type, the withdrawal from this environment where he does not have recourse to ample expression may be a defensive move. He changes his environment—transfers to a job better suited to his creative expression.

A soldier, on the other hand, who finds himself in an incompatible situation — the wrong outfit, the boring job, the remote location — often finds it impossible to change his circumstances with anywhere near the same ease as he might in civilian life. The nature of service organization and military policy do not allow this social and economic mobility. It is, of course, on account of the needs of national interest that his freedom to change his military assignment must be a secondary consideration; the enormous size of the military establishment makes it virtually impossible to satisfy this multitude of individual requirements, so that what is taken for granted in civilian life is often impossible for the man in uniform.

The soldier is left without social and economic mobility and free choice. As a matter of fact, the average soldier, or officer, may not recognize his dilemma (the blocking of his creativity in a particular job). This situation and its potential dangers to men and military organizations must be recognized by and resolved by them.

Fortunately, the services (by sheer accident, I am certain) have stumbled on a partial solution by the introduction of such helpful devices and programs as craftshops, amateur theatrical productions, suggestion boxes, religious activities, and various forms of officially organized and sponsored entertainment. However, good as these are, by and large, they channel creative energy into nonduty pursuits only.

Latent in every type of military command are many different kinds of people — some articulate, persuasive, and aggressive; some inarticulate, shy, and hesitant. The creative talents of almost all of these personnel, be they officers, enlisted men, or civilian engineers or other specialists, could be employed more effectively for the optimum functioning of each military command.

The solution to the problem of releasing creativity from the ranks lies with command. Here, all grades are responsible (including noncommissioned officers, who may, in fact, play an even more vital role than commissioned officers) for discerning the creative release requirements and then acting to meet them. There is no way to discern creativity and recognize immediately its fortunate possessors by methodical means. Therefore, to recognize it, one must have knowledge of the subject, act accordingly, and permit creativity to grow and seek expression.

A special word about the staff function is necessary. Staff officers should be first-rate creative people. Once the commander issues his decision, if he is a good commander, in the Nelson manner, he gives his staff wide latitude in its implementation. It is the responsibility of each one of the general and special staff officers or other staff types throughout the services to wield his creative ideas so as best to manage his respective staff responsibility. Each possesses a broad and deep association with his particular activity, which should lead to a wealth of intuitive and similarly creative products.

The same responsibility rests on civilian employees of the military services, be they in research and development or in administrative activities. Some of the most outstanding advances in weapons systems have been the result of the creative ideas of civilian engineers employed at government arsenals. The same concepts of creativity expounded herein for purely military applications have similar implications for civilians. Sympathetic supervisory military personnel can help to accelerate the quality and quantity of creativity used in the material research and development cycle, as well as in administration.

For instance, military intelligence is one of the staff functions that can be the most challenging to a creative mind, for it not only deals with extracting and establishing logistic, topographical, and other factual data about the enemy, it also allows one to accumulate knowledge about the behavior pattern of the enemy by observing him.

There are implications of the creative process that would call for a somewhat novel approach to the fundamental acquisition of knowledge by the intelligence officer. While not always true, creativity comes best from a man deeply immersed in his field of competence — in effect from a specialist. An intelligence officer is a specialist extraordinary.

This officer's creative role has some unusual twists to it. Through him the commander seeks information about, and estimates on, the enemy forces. This means, creatively speaking, whereas a deep and broad knowledge of friendly military forces is essential to good ideas in the other staff officers, this type of knowledge may be a deterrent to the intelligence officer. He must know his enemy or enemies of a particular war. In addition, since the enemy order of battle changes constantly, he must continually update data on units before him, their new formations, and different weapons. The enemy also is concealing and deceiving — taking every measure to make information absorption a difficult, challenging problem to overcome. The intelligence officer must work harder to acquire his information. His mind must be able, it would seem, to sift out chaff, to keep the essential character of the enemy in his subconscious, pure and uncompromised.

Theoretically, to the maximum degree feasible, intelligence officers must shut their minds to the torrent of information pouring into headquarters on their own forces and open them only to essential information on the enemy. If these principles are followed, the intelligence officer's brain, like a storage module of a computer, becomes packed with pure, raw data on the enemy, and he in essence will begin to produce what an enemy operations staff office would produce — creative ideas or intuitions which would probe deeply into the enemy general's brain and ultimately reach an intuition that reflected the enemy general's personality.

The sum of these techniques leads to the knack of insightful knowledge of how the enemy will act. It then follows that a commander must be able to recognize and actively seek an individual with unique capacities to perform this task. That is not to say that other areas of military activity are any the less creative, but intelligence work demands an unusual combination of skills that is found in very few men.

During disclosed investigation into the various natures of creative individuals, the nature of the creative process, the nature of the creative climate, and the inheritance from history on the subject, I have become increasingly aware of the need to make the idea of creativity known to the military services if for no other reason than to show how this creativity can be taken from the domain of theory and applied to the everyday activities of the military professions. It is not only uneconomical but it endangers national security to prevent the fruition of the best ideas or the development of the most creative people until a war demands them. Consequently, I would suggest as a minimum that a commander of men be aware of several factors.

1. He should be familiar with the elements of creativity, so that they may be recognized both in individuals of his command and by the commander within himself.

2. He should foster a suitable atmosphere in a command which is conducive to the development of creativity. In this respect the commander plays a key role. He has to extend a helping hand. He must recognize that to do this he needs a wide repertoire of skills. The skills include the ability to listen, an expectant readiness that he is about to hear something of significance, an ability to inspire, an ability to appeal, to disarm, to suggest. What will be needed to draw ideas from a particular creative individual will depend on that individual's personality; however, most important is the fact that the battle is best won if the commander possesses and expresses the sincere desire to understand and be helpful.

3. He must search for creative people. He, of course, must have some training and knowledge about the whole subject in order to do this; however, even then the problem will not be an easy one. While it will be easy enough to recognize some of the creative types quickly, these gifted men, probably downhearted and frustrated by previous experiences, criticized by disgruntled companions or supe-

riors and possibly by a few people who at least unconsciously hope that their schemes won't work in order that
their "I told you it wouldn't work" prophecies would be
validated, may have had their spirits quashed and need
buoying up. Others may have irked some commanders
because they have skipped channels to get the job done.
Frequently, the creative person possesses so much strength
on the surface that he seems to be one of the least likely to
need reassurance and nurturing, but he has really had so
little that it will help to give him some. Then again, many
of these people — bright, able, with plenty of good ideas —
are quiet, shy, introverted people who offer their brainchildren in such a hesitant fashion that they do not get a
proper hearing.

There are painters who are abstractionists, realists, sur-
realists, or cubists. In the field of military art there are as
many divisions as there are within the field of visual arts.
Some leaders are artists of the battlefield, some artists at
administration, some are best with the artistic medium of
tanks, others with logistics. Especially valuable on the
battlefield are those who excel in the ability to combine all
or several of the military art mediums.

We come to the same old cliché of the "square peg." It
seems that those in positions of responsibility should be
concerned in separating the military field into the several
branches of military art, and then sorting out leaders into
their respective groups according to their prospective artistic
talents.

Each soldier is creative to some degree, with his creativeness higher in some fields than others. In some way, each is
an artist. To the extent feasible, it would seem the height
of wisdom to place men where their artistic creativity would

be fulfilled so that we could get our highest art from each soldier and commander and extract the greatest value from our leadership dollar.

In conclusion, creative thinking is definitely a necessity in today's armed forces. To insure that military doctrine and tactics are abreast of existing technological advancements made through scientific research, creative thinking must be encouraged and developed. The complexities and wide dispersions required in modern warfare, whether atomic or guerrilla, highlight the need for thinking that transcends rote memory. For the individual officer, young or old, this means the application of his concerned efforts to seek improvements for current problems. For the senior, this means a tolerance of creative thinking by subordinates to allow them the opportunity to think creatively and to develop their individual abilities. For all members of the military this means adherence to a decision once rendered with the utmost loyalty and determination. Because it is so much easier for most people to be conformists, this means a determination to examine problems intelligently and a resolution to do the best possible to solve them. The superior must take maximum advantage of the collective thinking of his staff. The outstanding officer knows when to conform, but his primary goal should be continually to probe for new ideas and better solutions.

APPENDIX

The Command Decision

("The Command Decision" is a manuscript prepared originally for the Chief Historian, Headquarters, European Command in 1947 by Generaloberst Dr. Lothar Rendulic. General Rendulic commanded German forces during World War II. This account gives his "thoughts based on personal experience with particular reference to warfare in Russia."

The document is unusual because it is one of the rare instances where a commander discusses the thought processes of the leader in combat and then illustrates his points with personal experience. The reader will find many instances where General Rendulic dwells on the importance of a commander allowing full freedom for the exercise of the initiative of his subordinates, the foggy circumstances that habitually make the decision processes in combat more intuitional than mechanical, and the interlocking elements of the creative act and the materials that go into the creative sequence.

Interesting are his "longer breath" and his "command according to terrain." Every artist of note has had to persist with his own "longer breath" to see his idea to fruition. General Rendulic, convinced of the rationality and feel of his own idea, outlasted his enemy's thrusts and came out victorious.

Several paragraphs of the original manuscript are not included because they are not meaningful to the discussion of creativity in the application of military violence. All italics are textual unless otherwise noted.) — AUTHOR'S NOTE

The most difficult but also most crucial part of a commander's varied duties is the *making of a decision*....

The commander will consider the following *basic factors* in reaching a decision:

In many cases the mission he has received
In every instance the estimate of the situation and the
   terrain

This *mission* may be defined in a clear-cut and concise order that leaves the commander only little leeway in arriving at his decision. It may, on the other hand, also be couched in rather general terms which allow full freedom for personal initiative. Generally speaking, the more unequivocal and concise the order, the more easily the decision is reached. But even if an unequivocal and concise order has been received, situations which call for independent decisions will repeatedly arise during combat. In such situations the original, binding order becomes but a guiding principle. In Russia, orders very frequently had to be composed in rather broad terms mainly because of the vastness of the combat areas, and frequently also because maps were not very accurate.

The *estimate of the situation* includes our own situation, the enemy situation, the situation of the adjacent units, and — increasing in the same ratio as the freedom of action of the respective commander — also the general situation.

Our own situation: Prior to a military operation, our own situation usually is clear so long as the troops are stationary. Whenever troops are on the move, an advance estimate as to the time in which they will have covered, or will be able to cover, certain distances, might play a major role in the decision. Because of the lack of highways in Russia, and the serious effect of rain on the unimproved roads, it is not always possible to arrive at as accurate an estimate as in other parts of Europe. This is particularly true so far as motorized units are concerned.

During actual combat it is frequently very difficult to gain a clear view of our own situation fast enough. The troops themselves need a certain amount of time to evaluate their own situation and, even on a small scale, it is often not a simple matter to arrive at the correct picture. From corps level on down, quick appreciation of our own situation is particularly important because there is usually a need for immediate action, and the respective commander has only a limited amount of time to make his decision. . . .

The enemy situation: . . . The situation began to be obscure during the course of combat, during our own or enemy penetrations, and during counterattacks or breakthroughs. Entirely *new* situations arose in those instances. In Russia, tactical air reconnaissance of the enemy situation was faced by the same handicaps as have been mentioned above in connection with reconnaissance of our own situation.

In mobile warfare, division and corps headquarters generally had very little and sometimes no information at all prior to the actual clash with the enemy. In most instances, even higher headquarters had only very little background information on which to base their briefing of subordinate commands. The picture became somewhat clearer only after the clash. Whenever stabilized fronts developed into mobile warfare — be it that the enemy was thrown back or that we were withdrawing — the initial situation was much more easily determined because we knew the enemy forces which faced us then, and which would face us in the immediate future. . . .

Some uncertain factors which enter into a decision have

been discussed in the preceding paragraphs. There are, however, numerous other elements which may influence a commander in arriving at a decision. Their influence may be due either to their intangible nature, or to the difficulties which they entail.

One of the intangible elements in the attack is the *uncertainty as to* what *success* may be expected from the execution of planned measures. In the defense, intangible elements are the *uncertainty* about the *effectiveness of the enemy attack* and the ability of our own troops to contain it and, particularly, the extent to which other sectors may be weakened in favor of the sector in which the main effort is being made. Command and making of decisions would be very simple if it were possible to gauge these factors.

Moreover, difficulties arise whenever there are *several alternatives for the decision.* This is especially true whenever there is greater certainty of success on one hand, while on the other hand there is less certainty but, provided the action succeeds, promise for infinitely greater success. . . .

Many a man has a tendency to *attribute undue importance to influences* originating from various sources, particularly in difficult situations. This is especially true whenever such influences tend toward preventing the execution of a daring plan or toward the evasion of danger. In such cases, there always exists the promise of being able to avoid difficulties and of being relieved of a burden.

The personal traits of a commander may handicap him in reaching a decision, and may be responsible for errors of judgment on his part. There is many a man of weak and *vacillating character* who is unable to stand on his own feet. Even attempts at self-improvement have hardly any effect in such cases. At times, I encountered too much of an *analytical mind* in men of very high caliber. That type breaks given premises down until finally these and antitheses balance and cancel each other. Others, engulfed by the sea of uncertainty, cling to *slogans* such as "attack at any cost." Still others confuse *stubbornness* and *obstinacy* with *firmness*. Some people are particularly *careful* by nature and crave to be prepared for every eventuality. They will always play safe, but will seldom be successful. Finally, a particular danger lurks in *preconceived opinions*. Unless earlier experiences that are not applicable to the situation at hand play a role in them, they are usually formed on the basis of isolated facts contained in the mass of collected data.

There are, however, also personal traits which *greatly aid* the commander in reaching a decision. Spiritual power, strength of character, maturity of mind, and personal experience are particularly valuable assets in this respect. Self-appraisal and unceasing efforts at self-improvement are imperative for a commander. An important aspect of any personal experience is the fact that, during its course, the commander has had an opportunity for self-analysis. Out of the great variety of different temperaments and characters, the man with a *cool head and an aggressive spirit* has the best prerequisites for success. The other way around, things would work out badly.

A thorough education in strategy and tactics will equip the commander with a valuable foundation. It is not so much a matter of acquiring actual knowledge, as it is one of training the mind along lines of strategic and tactical thought and judgment. Such a training of the mind, therefore, must be made the goal of education.

Our *service regulations on strategy and tactics* are the crystallization of experiences gathered during past wars. They are, more specifically, crystallized experiences of always the most recent war, which in each instance are applied with a view toward a future war. In every new war, however, there always are phases which it has been impossible to foresee. I only need to call to the reader's mind the value attributed to the French fortifications and the failure of the French doctrine of command and combat, the difference between the vulnerability of flanks in France and Belgium in 1940 and in Russia in 1941, and finally, the importance assumed by aviation, tanks, and mines. Service regulations on strategy and — in their broad, fundamental outlines — also those on tactics, can and must for this reason be put only into *rather general terms.*

The German manual on strategy entitled "Truppen-führung" (operations) was written along very general lines. As a result, not many of the principles set forth therein can be said to have been completely superseded by events of the late war. Whenever we opened a manual at all during the war, our interpretation of its context changed from year to year because we always read it in light of current experiences. In peacetime we studied manuals from an altogether different, less knowing viewpoint. They were, however, good training aids. The operations manual mentioned only one definite figure, i.e., that a division in the attack deploys over three to four kilometers, and in the defense over six kilometers. These figures probably were due to the mental aftereffect of the war of position of 1915 to 1918, despite the fact that the manual had been expressly written for a war of movement. I had the opportunity of talking to one of the authors still prior to the outbreak of the late war, and asked him why these figures had been included in the otherwise very broad directive. He replied that, "these figures are nothing but basic references. We had to include some fundamental indication on which the application of the principles set forth in the manual could be based. Otherwise, somebody might conceive of attacking a front of from ten to fifteen kilometers with only one division."

It is easy to understand that such indications soon assume the character of a compelling concept, especially since during the course of his basic and advanced training every German commander had to execute many problems and exercises, all of which were consistently based on these indications. However, the war in Russia required a different method. The vast expanse of the area and the numerical superiority of the enemy forced us to apply methods of mobile warfare in which a division attacked on a front ten and more kilometers wide. In September of 1941, my division had to cover a sector of fifty kilometers width on the DESNA. In the defense, individual divisions had to be assigned a stretch of front of up to 40 kilometers (as, for instance, each one of the four divisions of my corps in the OREL area in 1943). Many of the commanders — and, gradually, certainly most of them — quickly adjusted themselves to the requirements.

Some, however, were unable to reconcile the glaring contradiction between these figures and those which they had learned and worked with for such a long time. To many, a mission in which an area by far greater than one indicated by the figures in the manual had been assigned, appeared doomed to failure or to be outright impossible, even though they were well aware of the fact that these figures did no longer apply in practice. The result, at any rate, was uncertainty. These commanders were greatly limited in their ability to make decisions. Such is the effect which may be brought about by including figures in a service regulation.

Although service regulations can *never* prescribe *how* decisions are to be reached, there are, nevertheless, certain *principles* which, in my opinion, can be applied in almost all situations and which *make it easier to reach a decision.* It is always necessary, however, for the commander to ascertain with great care whether the situation permits or precludes their application; otherwise, they assume the character of slogans. This reminds us of the old principle that, "in case of doubt, the *bolder decision* is the better one." But this applies only in the case where a real doubt exists as to which of two or more possibilities should be adopted. Whenever there is a certain possibility which, however, does not fully apply to the situation at hand, then not even its greater boldness constitutes a recommendation in its favor. As a matter of fact, in such an instance there *can* be no real doubt. More explicit details will be given in an example.

Another guiding principle to be followed in making a decision is that, whenever possible, the *initiative of action* must be ours; that is to say, our own intentions must be considered paramount to the observed or suspected intentions of the enemy. Never should a decision follow the trend of the enemy's measures. We must not permit enemy measures to divert us from our goal, unless they constitute a serious threat. During the course of a military operation, the key to success is frequently an unwavering *adherence* to our own purpose along the general line of the final decision. One must, however, avoid crossing the border line from firmness to inflexibility.

Closely related to the above guiding principle is an element which must be present in every decision, an element which I should like to call the "axiom of the *longer breath* in the last quarter-hour." War is not only a contest of weapons, but also a contest of will power. The contest of will power mounts relatively to the contest of weapons. Wherever the contest of weapons has reached a climax and the issue is about to be decided, or whenever all reserves are spent and the operation is about to enter a critical phase, the climax of the contest of will power must not always be allowed to coincide with that of the contest of weapons but must frequently be carried further. At the moment when the contest of weapons has reached its climax, the impact of influences originating from the situation and from other sources upon the commander is most severe. It is then — so to speak, during the last quarter hour — that the commander must remain firm to the last, calm, and resolute. The fact that the German Supreme Command of the Army failed during "the last quarter-hour" of the battle of the Marne in 1914 was the reason for our losing that battle, and probably the war as well. During the late war, too, many an operation was stopped by one side just as the enemy was about to reach an identical decision. I shall later on cite a small-scale example from the Russian campaign. . . .

One of the most important fundamental principles under-lying a decision is the following: The foremost thought in every decision concerning a strategic or tactical situation must be the *main effort*. So long as the commander concentrates on the main effort, he will be confronted by a more or less clear-cut problem. He will more easily be able to formulate his decision along a certain line. However, his problem in reaching a decision will be solved no further than this. The extent to which his task is facilitated is minute compared to the difficulties which arise in building the framework of the main effort. The main effort is one of the elements which determine the very nature of a decision. First to be decided are the location and the direction of the main effort. Since the size of available forces is never unlimited, the formulation of the main effort necessarily must be based on the premise that other sectors have to be weakened in favor of the main effort and the creation of reserves. Of course, there are limits to the extent to which sectors can be weakened. Consequently, there are limits to building the main effort. It is of the utmost importance that these limits be correctly evaluated. Here, the commander has a broad and rewarding field in which to apply the above-mentioned guiding principles pertaining to daring and personal initiative. Here, these guiding principles are almost always applied to advantage and will facilitate the making of decisions.

Terrain plays an important role in every decision. It is particularly important in commanding a tactical unit or a division, and frequently even a corps. In contrast to the rest of Europe, the terrain in Russia is rather monotonous. But here, too, there are — at least so far as tactical considerations are concerned — certain key positions, the possession of which is of far-reaching importance. In contrast to the only too frequently unclear picture of the general situation, maps used in conjunction with data collected by air reconnaissance and — in the more immediate vicinity — also by ground reconnaissance, impart a fairly accurate picture of at least the general character of the terrain. Both air and ground reconnaissance are particularly necessary in Russia. In view of the above-mentioned facts, there developed the practice of placing greater emphasis on reliable data in making a decision, and of ascribing almost all-exclusive importance to terrain whenever a situation was unclear. In this manner, many commanders developed the principle of "command according to terrain." There is no intention of stating that this principle is a poor one and should be rejected. In completely unclear situations it will frequently be impossible to do anything else prior to the encounter with the enemy. But whenever the situation is at least somewhat clear, it must be remembered in the attack that the enemy, too, will occupy key positions with particularly strong forces if he should reach them before we do, and that it cannot be to our advantage to direct our thrust against the enemy's very point of resistance which is strongest because it is based upon favorable terrain. We must break this main hostile resistance by means of other maneuvers. In defensive operations, we must remember before we decide about the disposition of our forces and about the zone for the reserves, that the Russians hardly ever attacked sectors which were strong by virtue of terrain and weapons, but that they frequently attempted break-throughs at unexpected points.

Finally, there is a great advantage in *knowing one's enemy*. Whenever the commander knows at least in a general way what he may expect of the command and the combat value of his opponent, it will be easier for him to make a decision. It is for this reason that the study of the enemy and of the individual traits of his commanders is so valuable.

If, in *summarizing*, we review the difficulties inherent in the very nature of the mobile warfare, and the various situations which may confront the commander prior to the initial encounter with the enemy, as well as those developing during the course of combat, we shall have to state that the basic elements underlying a decision always contain numerous factors whose bearing and importance is unknown. The enemy situation is not clear enough, a fact which frequently is true also of our own situation. The mission received by the commander will be couched in more general terms the more undetermined the situation. In addition, there are the above-mentioned handicaps which may spring from the nature of things and the personal characteristics of the commander.

And nevertheless a decision must be reached, even if it is fully realized that it will be but a shot in the dark. Clausewitz makes a statement to the effect that war is the realm of uncertainty, and that the only known quantities are the character and ability of the commander. As we have seen, this applies particularly to the making of decisions.

A decision, therefore, is not a *problem of simple arithmetic,* but a *creative act.* Even in instances in which a decision is not the outcome of lengthy deliberations, the way leading up to a decision involves a complicated mental process in which, among other factors, also the *temperament* of the individual finds expression. Intuition and a *keen sense of perception* play a considerable role. Even if the commander has a large quantity of reference material at his disposal, and even if he has sufficient time for careful evaluation of all known factors, it still remains true that *the process by which a decision is reached is, in the final analysis, nearly always a secret which, in most instances, remains insoluble even to the person who has arrived at the decision.*

Examples to the Study "The Command Decision"
(Attack and defense at ROGACHEV, July 1941)

On 14 July 1941, during the pursuit of the retreating Russians, two infantry divisions of the LIII Corps crossed the BERESINA at BOBRUJSK. A third division—the 52nd Infantry Division which I commanded — crossed the BERESINA at SWISLOTSCH. Of the two divisions to the south, the 267th[1] had ROGACHEV as its objective, the other division aimed at SLABIN (about 50 kilometers to the south). The 52nd Infantry Division was to march at first in the direction of MOGILEW. Approximately 30 kilometers ahead of the division advanced the rear elements of the XXIV Panzer Corps. At noon of 15 July, while advancing on a broad front, the 267th Infantry Division had engaged the enemy about 10 kilometers west of the DNJEPR and its tributary,[2] but had been unable to dislodge him. In the evening the enemy in turn attacked at several points. By evening of 15 July the 52nd Infantry Division had advanced to within 15 or 20 kilometers of MOGILEW. Having marched 35 kilometers, it proceeded to bivouac for the night along the road to advance. At about 2000 an Ordonnanzoffizier (junior adjutant) from corps brought an order, the gist of which was as follows: "West of the DNJEPR and its subsidiary, 267th Infantry Division has encountered strong enemy forces along both sides of the road to ROGACHEV, and is engaged in combat at that point. Left flank at A-village.[3] 52nd Infantry Division will break bivouac at once, proceed to the area west of OSERANY, assemble there, and hold itself in readiness for a thrust on ROGACHEV along the east bank of the tributary. One infantry regiment will march directly to A-village to support the 267th Infantry Division."

After a night march covering between 12 and 20 more kilometers, the bulk of the division reached the area west of OSERANY in the morning of 16 July. The 205th Infantry Regiment — the rear element of the division — and one battalion of light artillery were branched off to A-village. The Russians held OSERANY. After a brief encounter the

---

[1] I am not sure whether this is the correct number.

[2] I cannot recall the name of that river. In the following pages I shall call it the tributary.

[3] I cannot recall the name of the village.

enemy withdrew to the eastern bank of the tributary. Now the troops had to have some rest, at least until noon, since they had covered up to 55 kilometers within the past 24 hours. Upon leaving the woods west of OSERANY, one engineer company was attacked by a Russian bomber squadron and suffered a few casualties.

There was, of course, no telephone communication with corps in BOBRUJSK. Radio communications, which until then, and later on, too, never failed, did not function. A large wooded region through which we had marched, extended from the north up to a point in line with OSERANY. To the south, the west bank of the tributary far beyond the BOBRUJSK-ROGACHEV road consisted of open, flat terrain covered with wheat fields. The following measures were taken next: Reconnaissance across the tributary in easterly direction and in the direction of ROGACHEV, then in southerly direction. Dispatch of an officer for establishing communications with the troops near A-village; the command post of the 267th Infantry Division was unknown. Dispatch of an officer with situation report to corps. Construction of a bridge across the tributary at OSERANY by using a floating bridge which had washed ashore on the near bank of the river. Military bridging equipment was not available. The tributary was about 60 meters wide and only 1 meter deep at that point; that is to say, it could be forded.

The combat patrol which had been sent out beyond OSERANY encountered enemy forces about 3 kilometers east of that place. The patrol was unable to determine the enemy's strength in the woods, and advanced no farther. Soon thereafter an enemy battery opened fire on OSERANY. The combat patrol was reinforced and a light artillery battalion committed to action. At about 1000 the first reconnaissance report arrived from the unit in the south. It read approximately as follows: "Severe fighting at A-village, Hamlets B and C (situated east of A-village toward the river) occupied by enemy forces. No other hostile forces west of the tributary. From the eastern bank fire from several machine guns." Soon, thereafter, the liaison officer which had been sent to the troops at A-village reported as follows: "Violent fighting from A-village on to the south. Enemy reinforcing. Own 205th Regiment arrived just in time. Elements already committed in counterthrust south of A-village." After 1100 a junior adjutant from the regiment of the 267th Infantry Division arrived and orally reported as follows: "Enemy pressure is constantly increasing. The situation is very tense. The regiment requests support. Its division has no more forces at its disposal." Strangely enough, hardly any battle noise from the south was to be heard within the 52nd Division sector, although the distance to the combat zone amounted only to from 12 to 15 kilometers. (Wind direction)

THE TWO ALTERNATIVES It seemed to me that the situation no longer permitted a wait for orders from corps, particularly since the troops had had a minimum of the rest they needed. Noon rations were just being distributed. Naturally, I had been pondering over the situation throughout the morning. At first, my deliberations centered on that part of the corps order which indicated the intention of thrusting east of the tributary toward ROGACHEV. It was one way in which to relieve pressure on our forces fighting on the west bank of the subsidiary. It was, indeed, the *"strategic"* solution which, should it succeed, might have a very far-reaching effect; which, by its very nature, would make itself felt far beyond merely relieving the forces fighting in the south. The very first combat-patrol reports, however, revealed that success was highly problematic for the following two reasons: First of all, the undetermined enemy situation on the east bank of the tributary, which could be clarified only by throwing stronger forces into action. Secondly, the largely wooded terrain and the fact that under prevailing circumstances the division was not strong enough for such a far-reaching operation.

As the situation of our forces to the south continued to be clarified, I found my estimate confirmed. It became more and more apparent that the situation of these forces demanded a very early relief of pressure. For that purpose, the *tactical* solution presented itself. Calling for a direct thrust south, into the flank of the attacking enemy, it tackled the problem at its core with a view toward achieving a success more limited in scope, but all the more certain. The first, "strategic," alternative played a considerable role in my deliberations for a rather prolonged period of time because it was the more daring, and because a unilateral deviation from what I knew to be the intention of corps was more difficult for me than an unprejudiced decision would have been. Nevertheless, the bolder and, if successful, more promising alternative had to be set aside in favor of the other because of the above-mentioned reasons. Barring the corps order and the intention it indicated, the final decision would have been so self-evident as to obviate any "genuine doubt" . . . about which alternative to adopt. Certainly, no such doubt could ever have arisen as late as shortly before noon. After all, the "strategic" solution conformed neither to the situation in the south nor to our own strength.

About noon, I therefore decided to gather all available forces and to thrust south into the flank of the attacking enemy, leaving the reconnaissance battalion at OSERANY as our rear guard and for further reconnaissance. Elements of the division were moved into assembly positions in such a manner that the advance could get under way at 1300.

Shortly before 1300 an officer arrived from corps, bringing me the order, dated 1000, immediately to launch attack to the south. He had driven over the highway leading to MOGILEW, and then had used the road through the woods previously traveled by the division. On the latter stretch his vehicle repeatedly bogged down in the swampy ground.

Notwithstanding the repeated exchange of information and the fact that we were in communication with our forces in action, the attack was a venture into complete uncertainty.[4] We only knew in general that a considerably superior enemy of unknown strength was attacking our own forces. We knew nothing at all about the situation in the nearby sector east of the tributary. The division was short one-third of its infantry and one-fourth of its artillery. And despite all this, I can hardly remember to have been more confident during any other of the many attacks I led.

I shall omit the details of the attack. By nightfall, the 52nd Infantry Division had broken through the defense front in the Russian north flank to a depth of from two to four kilometers. The only elements unable to make any progress were those attacking on the left flank in the vicinity of the tributary. They were being held up by exceedingly heavy flanking fire from machine guns, mortars, and guns emplaced on the eastern bank of the river, which could not be silenced. Still, during the night of 16-17 July the enemy situation became more clear. Statements made by prisoners belonging to three infantry divisions indicated that since the morning of 16 July the one and one-half regiments of the 267th Infantry Division north of the big highway were being attacked by two divisions. Since the

[4] Air reconnaissance was available neither on that nor the following days.

morning of 16 July a third division had crossed the tributary by the northern bridge.[5] Contrary to original plans, however, this division was not employed in an attack to the west. Instead, as soon as the enemy discovered rather strong German forces west of OSERANY, it was diverted to the north flank where by 1700 it had just formed a defense front between A-village and the tributary, i.e., at a right angle to the attack front, when the attack of the 52nd Infantry Division got under way.

The attack was contained on 17 July and the 205th Infantry Regiment brought into action. Our forces advanced 12 kilometers to the south, but no longer in a flanking direction, and pushed the enemy back about 4 kilometers to the east. Now the 52nd Infantry Division had to take over the front from the tributary to about one kilometer south of the highway. The elements of the 267th Infantry Division had suffered severe casualties and had been unable to participate in the attack. They were removed to their division south of the highway.

The division prepared for the defense. It was spread along a line of sixteen kilometers. Neither terrain nor enemy situation offered any clue as to a point of main effort. Because of the far-flung line which the division had to hold, all three infantry regiments were employed. One of them was assigned a smaller sector, but had to provide one battalion as division reserve at the big highway. The engineer battalion, which was working in the lines during the day, was located halfway between the highway and A-village. An additional division reserve was stationed in the vicinity of A-village. It consisted of 3 bicycle companies

---

[5] The bridge and the troop movements over it could not be observed from the ground.

and the reconnaissance battalion less its cavalry troop. The reconnaissance battalion could be moved closer to the front because the enemy forces east of OSERANY had disappeared and the area to the east was free of enemy forces up to the railroad line. Only in southerly direction, after an advance of about five kilometers toward ROGACHEV, did the patrols encounter hostile forces which they were unable to penetrate. The cavalry troop was left in Oserany for security and reconnaissance missions. On 19 July one heavy artillery regiment with two battalions (150-mm. medium howitzers and 105-mm. guns, a total of six batteries) was assigned to the division. Air reconnaissance was still not available.

The Russian large-scale attack started on 20 or 21 July. The positions completed by that time consisted of simple trenches. There were no obstacles because wire was one of the unavailable items. Russian fire lasting for several hours had begun in the morning and covered the entire front as far as several kilometers south of the highway. The main target area, although cleverly screened by the enemy, nevertheless appeared to extend from a point southeast of A-village to several kilometers south of the latter. The Russians revealed themselves in possession of a surprisingly large amount of heavy artillery which fired very accurately. Ammunition appeared to be no problem.

During the first days of the fighting a news item which had appeared in the British press became known, according to which the Russians under the command of Marshal Timoschenko had launched an offensive aimed at the rear and the communications of the German Army Group advancing in Central Russia. A comparison of events and information received from other front sectors could not

but leave the impression that the main effort of Timoschenko's offensive had hit the 52nd Infantry Division.

I shall omit the details of the fighting. The enemy repeatedly shifted his main effort within the area from a point
about 2 kilometers north of the highway to the region
southeast of A-village. Prisoner statements revealed that
there were always three divisions on the attack within this
area, and that all losses they suffered during the day were
replaced during the following night. Some of the heavy batteries belonged to the Moscow School of Artillery which had
recently arrived with 20 of its heavy batteries. At the points of
main effort the Russian infantry attacked according to a system of waves, each from four to five ranks deep. Wave
after wave appeared in order to keep the attack rolling—
a clumsy and expensive method, but one very likely con-
sistent with the character of the Russian infantry. Not even
during nighttime did the Russian artillery reduce its fire
more than slightly. As a result, it was not always possible
to get enough supplies to the infantry on the line. The
weather was hot and sunny throughout the operation.

THE INFLUENCE EXERCISED BY THE SUPERIOR OFFICER The
battle continued with undiminished fury. On the fourth day,
as on the preceding ones, the Commanding General of the
Corps came to my command post at about lunch time. In
the meantime, the situation of the division had developed
as follows: The infantry had suffered severe casualties.
Individual companies had been decimated to such an extent
that they had to be dissolved. Most of them had lost from
one-third to one-half of their men. One-third of the machine
guns had been knocked out. Because of enemy hits or
excessive wear and tear, not one of the batteries had all of
its 4 guns left; one-third of the batteries had only two guns
left, two batteries had only one. The troops had reorganized

reserves repeatedly, but all of these had been used up. I had just assigned for commitment the one company which had been detached that same morning from the regiment on the right flank. That regiment had suffered comparatively the least losses so far, and I had already withdrawn one battalion from it at an earlier time. In this situation the Commanding General told me (as to meaning): "If you believe that you cannot hold out any longer, I leave it up to you to decide whether you want to withdraw the division to a line running along A-creek or even to the BERESINA. In the latter case, BOBRUJSK will have to be held as a bridgehead. If your division is torn apart in this action, it will be useless for some time to come, and the approach to BOBRUJSK will not be covered."

I must admit that up to that moment the thought of requesting the withdrawal of the division had never entered my mind. Now I had been given the authority for its withdrawal without ever having asked for it myself, and together with that authority had been charged with added responsibility. I knew that all troops of Fourth Army already were east of the DNJEPR. It was, to be sure, not part of my responsibility to be concerned about who would cover the lines of communication of Fourth Army after a withdrawal of my division left them unprotected. Nevertheless, I was able completely to dismiss that thought from my mind. Just the same, my mission called for covering the approach to BOBRUJSK under any and all circumstances if the present position should become untenable. I had to hold the BERESINA with a bridgehead somewhere between its east bank and my present position. Considering the superior enemy forces, it was open to doubt whether the mission could be accomplished with a division that had been forced to yield ground in combat and was out of touch with its units.

I rejected the thought of a withdrawal. My decision was based on the confidence I had in my men—badly weakened and completely exhausted as they were—and their commanders, all of whom I knew well and had come to know even better during the recent fighting. Moreover, the knowledge gained about the enemy and his methods of attack played a role that lent me a certain amount of encouragement. These, however, were only two of the elements entering into my decision. For the rest, I would have been unable to justify my decision in all of its details. It was more a matter of conviction, impossible to prove, that the position could be held after all, and of unwavering determination to hold it. *Quite possibly the decisive factor was, however, that indefinable feeling which in the last analysis we cannot rationalize* [author's italics]. One fact, though, became clear to me: not easy to begin with, my decision became much more difficult upon the authorization given me.

The above-mentioned experience taught me that a superior must never communicate his apprehensions to a subordinate, and that he must never unload part of his own responsibility on him. Increased responsibility undoubtedly can bolster the feeling of self-reliance of a commander, and consequently also his strength. But such an involved psychological experiment, the outcome of which is never certain, must not be conducted in the midst of a critical situation.

THE "LONGER BREATH" In the afternoon of that day a trench sector of more than 400 meters had to be abandoned. We were forced to make the best of it. During the night small groups of from eight to ten men were being pulled out here and there by the battalions and regiments in order to form a reserve. The chance for forming a division reserve was long past. In conducting further operations I was limited to communicating with the regimental commanders and to adapting artillery fire to tactical situations. On the following morning the Russian attacks resumed with undiminished fury. By means of concentrated artillery fire we succeeded several times in breaking up enemy attack waves and enemy battalions in assembly position. We lost two more trench sectors of considerable length, and the enemy exploited his success of the previous day to a depth of one kilometer. During the course of the day, also individual commanders finally began to report with particular emphasis on the serious state of exhaustion of their men. These had not slept for days, and, despite the brutal summer heat, could not even be regularly supplied with water. Gunners even fell asleep while servicing their pieces. On that day our planes finally flew reconnaissance missions. They spotted no new enemy forces east of the DNJEPR. That fact, however, would not necessarily have to mean anything very important since extensive woodlands covered the terrain and the Russians were masters at concealment from air reconnaissance. Up to that time, we had taken prisoners belonging to five infantry divisions. Three of those divisions had been positively identified as totally committed; of the other two we had identified at least elements in combat.

In the late afternoon I found myself compelled to tackle the same problem that had confronted me the previous day: I had to make a decision. Only this time it was still more difficult. From the unit reports I was able to deduct that the enemy, who on that day attacked with particular disregard for his own losses, must have suffered a huge number of casualties. The air reconnaissance report, too, took on certain significance. Exhaustion and casualties among our own troops had further increased. Nevertheless—I reminded myself—there must, after all, be a limit also to the enemy's ability of sustaining the attack. I resolved to hold the position through the next day as well. From my point of view I was waging a contest of will power. I could do but little in furthering the contest of weapons.

I admit that I awaited the following day with great suspense. That day brought the surprise: Dawn broke and —only slight enemy artillery activity; absolute quiet reigned in the enemy positions. The day passed without a Russian attack. And none came until, on 15 August, we ourselves resumed the offensive under different strategic circumstances.

My decision of the last evening of the defense battle proved that I had the "longer breath in the last quarter-hour." . . .

Notes

CHAPTER I

[1]Lin Piao, "Lin Piao's Manifesto," *Army* (December 1965), pp. 47-51, taken from the Red Chinese *Peking Review* (No. 36) (September 3, 1965), compiled and condensed by Dr. Fritz G. A. Kreamer for *Army*.

[2]Robert Payne, *Mao Tse-tung, Ruler of Red China* (New York: Henry Schuman, 1950), p. 273.

CHAPTER II

[1]Nathaniel Cheairs Hughes, Jr., *General William J. Hardee— Old Reliable* (Baton Rouge: Louisiana State University Press, 1965), pp. 41-50.

[2]Allen Wescott, *Mahan on Naval Warfare* (London: Sampson Low, Marston & Co., Ltd., 1919), p. 13.

[3]Oscar Koch, Letter to Colonel Mrazek (June 17, 1968).

[4]William D. Puleston, *Mahan, The Life and Works of Captain Alfred Thayer Mahan, U.S.N.* (New Haven: Yale University Press, 1939), p. 297.

[5]*Ibid.*, pp. 297–8.

[6]Napoleon Bonapart, *Memoirs of the History of France During the Reign of Napoleon,* dictated by the Emperor at Saint Helene to the Count de Montholon. *Historical Miscellanies*, English translation (London: Henry Coburn & Co. and Martin Bossange & Co., 1823), p. 89.

CHAPTER III

[1]Omar N. Bradley, "Leadership," *Military Review* (September 1966), p. 48.

[2]*Ibid.*

[3]Matthew B. Ridgway, "Leadership," *Military Review* (October 1966), p. 40.

[4]Lev Nikolaevich Tolstoi, *What Is Art?*, trans. Aylmer Muade (London: Oxford Press, World's Classics, 1959), p. 51.

[5]*Ibid.*, p. 61.

[6]I. E. Mouromtseff, "Who Is the True Inventor?" *Institute of Radio Engineers Proceedings* XXXVIII (June 1950), p. 610.

[7]David Ogilvy, *Confessions of an Advertising Man* (New York: Atheneum, 1963).

[8]*Ibid.*

[9]R. N. Ashen, ed., *Freedom. Its Meaning* (New York: Harcourt, Brace & Co., Inc., 1940), p. 383.

[10]Robert Lee Scott, *Flying Tiger* (New York: Doubleday & Co., 1959), p. 10.

[11]W. Somerset Maugham, *The Summing Up* (New York: Doubleday & Co., 1938).

[12]A. T. Mahan, *Life of Nelson* (Boston: Little, Brown & Co., 1918), I, p. 312.

[13]*Ibid.*

CHAPTER IV

[1]M. Yasyukov, "Soviet Armed Forces Place Special Emphasis on Initiative and Ingenuity," (*Navy* title and translated from an article by Lt. Col. M. Yasyukov in *Kommunist Voorushennykh Sil,* Moscow, no date or page given by *Navy*) *Navy* (December 1963), p. 36. Editor makes comment, "With recurrent criticism that the Pentagon is stifling the initiative and ingenuity of our commanding generals and admirals, NAVY believes its readers might like to see how the Soviet Union rates these characteristics in its combat leaders."

[2]Edmund W. Sinnott, "The Creativeness of Life," Harold H. Anderson, ed., *Creativity and Its Cultivation* (New York: Harper & Row, 1959), p. 23.

[3]Eliot D. Hutchinson, *How to Think Creatively* (New York: Abingdon, 1949), p. 28.

[4]Clark Lee and Richard Henschel, *Douglas MacArthur* (New York: Henry Holt, 1952), p. 201.

[5]Lothar Rendulic, *"The Command Decision"* (Prepared for the

Chief Historian, Headquarters European Command, 1947), p. 17.

[6]Bernard Law Montgomery, Viscount of Alamein, *The Path to Leadership* (New York: G. P. Putman's Sons, 1961), p. 51.

[7]Sinnott, *op. cit.*, p. 24.

[8]Will Durant, *The Story of Philosophy* (New York: Pocket Books, Inc., 1954), p. 337. See also, Arthur Schopenhauer, *The Works of Schopenhauer*, ed. by Will Durant (New York: Simon & Schuster, 1928), pp. 105, 6 and ff.

[9]William James, *Pluralistic Universe* (New York and London: Longman's, 1909), p. 212.

[10]M. B. Parloff and J. H. Handlon, "The Influence of Criticalness on Creative Problem-Solving in Dyads," *Psychiatry* XXVII Number 1 (February 1964), p. 17.

[11]H. W. Carr, *Henri Bergson* (London: Thomas Nelson & Sons, Ltd., 1919), p. 46.

[12]Frank Barron, "The Psychology of Imagination," *Scientific American* (September 1958), CIC, p. 164.

[13]Karl von Clausewitz, *On War*, trans. by O. J. Matthijs Jolles (Washington: The Infantry Journal Press, 1950), p. 42.

[14]*Ibid.*, pp. 32, 33.

[15]*Ibid.*, p. 33.

[16]*Ibid.*, pp. 84-5.

[17]*Ibid.*, p. xxxi.

[18]Alfred T. Mahan, *Naval Strategy* (Boston: Little, Brown & Co., 1911), p. 299.

[19]Thomas Edward Lawrence, *The Seven Pillars of Wisdom* (New York: Doubleday & Co., 1947), Dell paperback edition, p. 191.

[20]*Ibid.*, p. 197.

[21]*Ibid.*, p. 194.

[22]*Ibid.*, p. 195.

CHAPTER V

[1]Will Durant, *The Story of Civilization: Part II, The Life of Greece* (New York: Simon & Schuster, 1939), pp. 541-2.

[2]*Ibid.*, p. 538.

[3]*Ibid.*, p. 539.

[4]*Ibid.*, p. 540.

[5]Durant, *The Story of Civilization: Part III, Caesar and Christ* (New York: Simon & Schuster, 1944), p. 48.

[6]*Ibid.*, p. 50.

[7]*Ibid.*, p. 51.

[8]Harold Lamb, *Hannibal* (New York: Doubleday & Company, 1958).

[9]Earl Wavell, *Soldiers and Soldiering* (London: Jonathan Cape, 1953), p. 107.

[10]Theodore Ayrault Dodge, *Great Captains, Napoleon* (Boston: Houghton Mifflin, 1907), IV, pp. 674-5.

[11]*Ibid.*, I, pp. 139-40.

[12]*Ibid*, IV, p. 686.

[13]*Ibid.*, I, p. 441.

[14]*Ibid.*

[15]Napoleon I, Emperor of the French, *Napoleon and Modern War; His Military Maxims* revised and annotated by Conrad H. Lanza (Harrisburg, Pa.: Military Service Publishing Company, 1943), p. 122.

[16]*Ibid.*, p. 147.

[17]*Ibid.*, pp. 147-8.

[18]Dodge, *op. cit.*, pp. 169-70.

[19]*Ibid.*, p. 170

[20]Alfred H. Barr, Jr., *What Is Modern Painting?* (Garden City: The Museum of Modern Art, 1956), p. 10.

[21]J. F. C. Fuller, *Decisive Battles* (New York: Harper & Bros., 1942), p. 680.

[22]John Allen Wyeth, *That Devil Forrest* (New York: Harper & Brothers, 1959), p. 564.

[23]Charles A. Willoughby and John Chamberlain, *MacArthur 1941-1951* (New York: McGraw-Hill Book Company, 1954), p. 7.

[24]*Ibid.*

CHAPTER VI

[1]S. S. Robison and Mary L. Robison, *A History of Naval*

Tactics from 1530 to 1930 (Annapolis: U.S. Naval Institute, 1942), p. 881.

[2]Alfred T. Mahan, *Types of Naval Officers* (Boston: Little, Brown & Company, 1918), p. 138.

[3]*Ibid.*

[4]C. J. Britton, *New Chronicles of the Life of Lord Nelson* (Birmingham, England: Cornish Brothers, 1946), p. 79.

[5]James R. Thursfield, *James R. Nelson and Other Naval Studies* (New York: E. P. Dutton, 1920), pp. 82-3.

[6]Alfred T. Mahan, *Life of Nelson* (Boston: Little, Brown & Co., 1918), I, p. 225.

[7]Alfred T. Mahan, *Admiral Farragut* (New York: Appleton & Company, 1892), pp. 318, 319.

[8]Theodore Taylor, *The Magnificent Mitscher* (New York: Norton & Company, 1954), p. 9.

[9]U.S.S. Enterprise Reports of July 3, 1944 (Washington, D.C.: Office, Chief of Naval History), p. 340.

[10]CTF (Command Task Force) 58 (Vice Admiral Mitscher) Action Report, September 11, 1944 (Washington, D.C.: Office, Chief of Naval History), p. 27.

[11]Enterprise, *op. cit.* p. 344.

[12]CTF 58 Report, *op. cit.*

[13]*Ibid.*

[14]Arliegh A. Burke, "Interview of Commander Arliegh A. Burke U.S.N. on the Battle of Empress of Augustus Bay," (Washington Office, Chief Naval History) (July 31, 1945), Number 411-1, p. 20.

[15]Arliegh A. Burke, "Action Report of Night Engagement off Cape Moltke on Night of November 1st–2nd, 1943," COMDESRON 23, Serial 012, November 1943 (Washington: Office, Chief of Naval History), p. 29.

[16]Howard Bucknell, "Give of Yourself, Captain," U.S. Naval Institute *Proceedings* (June 1964), Vol. 90, Number 6, p. 73.

CHAPTER VII

[1]Edward L. Beach, *Submarine* (New York: Holt, 1952), p. 5.

[2]*Ibid.*

[3]*Ibid.*

[4]*Ibid.*

[5]*Ibid.*

[6]W. G. Carr, *By Guess and By God* (London: Hutchinson & Co., n.d.), p. x.

[7]Wolfgang Frank, *The Sea Wolves,* trans. by R. O. B. Long (New York: Ballantine Books, 1955), p. 63.

[8]Nicholas Monsarrat, *The Cruel Sea* (New York: Alfred A. Knopf, Inc., 1951), p. 154.

[9]Theodore Roscoe, *United States Submarine Operations in World War II* (Annapolis: U.S. Naval Institute, 1949), p. 495.

[10]*Ibid.*

[11]J. H. Maurer, *Report of War Patrol Number One — U.S.S. ATULE (SS403),* Report SS403/A16/ASerial 013 (Arlington, Va.: Office of the Chief of Naval History, December 11, 1944), p. 10.

[12]J. H. Maurer, Personal interview (Pentagon: May 8, 1964).

[13]J. H. Maurer, Report, *op. cit.,* pp. 10, 11.

[14]J. H. Maurer, Personal interview, *op. cit.*

[15]Beach, *op. cit.,* p. 227.

[16]*Ibid.,* p. 228.

[17]*Ibid.*

[18]*Ibid.*

[19]*Ibid,* p. 200.

[20]Charles Lockwood and Hans Christian Adamson, *Through Hell and Deep Water* (New York: Chilton, 1956), p. 127.

[21]*Ibid.,* p. 247.

[22]*Ibid.*

[23]*Ibid.,* pp. 213-4

[24]S. D. Dealey, *Report of War Patrol Number Three—U.S.S. HARDER* (Washington, D.C.: Office of the Chief of Naval History, November 19, 1943), p. 8.

[25]*Ibid.*

[26]Roscoe, *op. cit.,* p. 337.

[27]Beach, *op. cit.,* p. 224.

[28]Roscoe, *op. cit.,* 463.
[29]*Ibid.*
[30]*Ibid.*

CHAPTER VIII

[1]Alex F. Osborn, *Developments in the Creative Education Movement,* based on an address at the 8th Annual Creative Problem Solving Institute at the University of Buffalo (Buffalo: undated), p. 1.

[2]Harold H. Anderson, "Creativity in Perspective," *Creativity and Its Cultivation,* Harold H. Anderson, ed. (New York: Harper & Row, 1959), p. 267.

[3]James R. Thursfield, *Nelson and Other Naval Studies* (New York: E. P. Dutton, 1920), p. 82.

[4]Frazier Hunt, *The Untold Story of Douglas MacArthur* (New York: Devin-Adair, 1954), pp. 122-3.

[5]Beach, *op. cit.,* p. 263.

[6]Eugene E. Jennings, *Anatomy of Leadership* (New York: Harper & Row, 1960), p. 151.

[7]James H. Ward, *Manual of Naval Tactics* (New York: D. von Nostrand & Company, 1859), p. 5.

[8]Gabriel Darrieus and René Daveluy, *War on the Sea,* trans. by Phillip R. Alger (Annapolis: U.S. Naval Institute, 1920), p. 68.
[9]*Ibid.*

CHAPTER IX

[1]Maxwell D. Taylor, "Some Reflections on the Subject of Leadership," from an address to students, the Citadel, 1956, taken from *Military Leadership* (West Point: United States Military Academy, 1960), 89-97, p. 95.

[2]Theodore Taylor, *op. cit.,* p. 26.

[3]John A. Wyeth, *op. cit.,* p. 563.

[4]Charles W. Thayer, *Guerrilla* (New York: Harper & Row, 1963), p. 61.

[5]*Ibid.*

[6]*Ibid.,* pp. 61-2.

[7]*Ibid.*, pp. 62-3.

[8]E. P. Potter and Chester W. Nimitz,eds., *Sea Power: A Naval History* (Englewood Cliffs, N.J.: Prentice-Hall, 1960), p. 9.

CHAPTER X

[1]Mao Tse-tung, *On Guerrilla Warfare,* trans. by Samuel B. Griffith (New York: Frederick A. Praeger, 1961), p. 3.

[2]Haldore Hanson, *Humane Endeavour* (New York: Farrar & Rinehart, Inc., 1939), p. 220.

[3]Thomas Edward Lawrence, *op. cit.*, p. 191.

[4]*Ibid.*, p. 195.

[5]*Ibid.*, p. 194.

[6]*Ibid.*, p. 198.

[7]*Ibid.*, p. 195.

[8]*Ibid.*, p. 197.

[9]T. W. Adams, "Creativity Conflict: Management versus Scientists," *Army Research and Development Newsmagazine* (August, 1963), IV, 1, p. 30.

[10]Michael Drury, "Of Course You're Creative!" *Glamour* (February, 1959), p. 91.

[11]Lawrence, *op. cit.*, p. 196.

[12]Lin Piao, *"Manifesto," op. cit.*, p. 48.

[13]*Ibid.*

[14]*Ibid.*

[15]*Ibid.*

[16]*Ibid.*

[17]*Ibid.*, p. 49

[18]*Ibid.*

[19]*Ibid.*, p. 50

CHAPTER XI

[1]Parloff and Handlon, *op. cit.*

[2]Alex F. Osborn, *Applied Imagination* (New York: Charles Scribner's Sons, 1963), p. 212.

[3]"Lincoln and Modern America," *Time* (May 10, 1963), p. 20.

[4]Arthur Koestler, *The Act of Creation* (New York: Macmillan Company, 1964), p. 117.

[5]*Ibid.*

[6]Henri Bergson, *Creative Evolution,* trans. by Arthur Mitchell (New York: Modern Library, 1944), p. 211.

[7]Harold Lasswell, "The Social Setting of Creativity," Anderson, *op. cit.,* p. 215.

[8]Mark S. Watson, "Control of the Military," *Ordnance* (November-December, 1962), p. 289.

[9]*Ibid.*

[10]Lockwood and Adamson, *op. cit.,* p. 72.

[11]William Grigg, "That Headstrong Kid Is Geared to Succeed," Washington *Evening Star* (May 5, 1946), p. A-1.

[12]*Ibid.*

[13]*Ibid.*

[14]*Ibid.*

[15]*Ibid.*

[16]Harold F. Harding, "Place of Creativity in the Military Mission," Military Creative Problem Solving Seminar (Fort Belvoir: U.S. Army Management School, March 1961), p. 53.

[17]Paul Nitze, "Brains in the Navy," *The Washington Post* (June 1, 1964), p. A-18.

Bibliography

BOOKS

ANDERSON, HAROLD H. (ed.). *Creativity and Its Cultivation.*
New York: Harper & Row, 1959.

ASHEN, R. N. (ed.). *Freedom. Its Meaning.* New York:
Harcourt, Brace & Co., Inc., 1940.

BEACH, EDWARD L. *Submarine.* New York: Holt, 1952.

BERGSON, HENRI. *The Creative Mind.* London, 1934.

————. *Creative Evolution.* Translated by Arthur Mitchell.
New York: Modern Library, 1944.

BONAPART, NAPOLEON. *Memoirs of the History of France During
the Reign of Napoleon.* Dictated by the Emperor at Saint
Helena to the Count de Montholon, *Historical Miscellanies,*
English translation. London: Henry Coburn & Co., 1823.

————. Napoleon I, Emperor of the French. *Napoleon and
Modern War; His Military Maxims.* Revised and annotated by
Conrad H. Lanza. Harrisburg, Pa.: Military Service Publishing
Company, 1943.

BRADFORD, ERNLE. *The Wind Commands Me.* New York:
Harcourt, Brace & World, Inc., 1965.

BRITTON, C. J. *New Chronicles of the Life of Lord Nelson.*
Birmingham, England: Cornish Brothers, 1946.

BUELL, AUGUSTUS C. *Paul Jones, Founder of the American Navy,
A History.* New York: Charles Scribner's Sons, 1906.

CARR, H. W. *Henri Bergson.* London:
Thomas Nelson & Sons, Ltd., 1919.

CARR, WILLIAM GUY. *By Guess and By God.* London:
Hutchinson & Co., Ltd., n.d.

————. *Good Hunting.* London: Hutchinson & Co., Ltd., 1940.

CLAUSEWITZ, KARL VON. *On War*. Translated by O. J. Matthijs Jolles. Washington, D.C.: Infantry Journal Press, 1950.

DARRIEUS, GABRIEL AND RENÉ DAVELUY. *War on the Sea*. Translated by Phillip R. Alger. Annapolis: U.S. Naval Institute, 1920.

DAVENPORT, CHARLES BENEDICT. *Naval Officers, Their Heredity and Development*. Washington, D.C.: Carnegie Institute, 1919.

DODGE, THEODORE A. *Great Captains, Napoleon*. Four volumes. Boston: Houghton Mifflin Company, 1904-07.

DURANT, WILL. *The Story of Civilization, Part II: The Life of Greece* and *Part III: Caesar and Christ*. New York: Simon & Schuster, 1939 and 1944.

————. *The Story of Philosophy*. New York: Pocket Books, Inc., 1954. See also Arthur Schopenhauer, *The Works of Schopenhauer*, ed. by Will Durant. New York: Simon & Schuster, 1928.

DYER, FREDERICK G. AND JOHN M. *Bureaucracy Versus Creativity*. Coral Gables: University of Miami Press, 1965.

FARAGO, LADISLAS. *The Tenth Fleet*. New York: Paperback Library, 1962.

FRANK, WOLFGANG. *The Sea Wolves*. New York: Ballantine Books, 1955.

FREDERICK II (Frederick the Great). *Instructions for His Generals*. Translated by T. R. Phillips. Harrisburg, Pa.: Military Service Publishing Company, 1944.

FREYTAG-LORINGHOVEN, HUGO VON. *The Power of Personality in War*. Translated by Oliver O. Spaulding. Harrisburg, Pa.: Military Service Publishing Company, 1955.

FULLER, J. F. C. *Decisive Battles*. New York: Harper & Bros., 1942.

GALLERY, DANIEL V. *2,000,000 Tons Under the Sea*. Chicago: Henry Reinhold Company, 1956.

GHISELIN, BREWSTER (ed.). *The Creative Process*. Berkeley: University of California Press, 1952; also New York: New American Library (Mentor Books), 1955.

HALE, JOHN R. *Famous Sea Fights from Salamis to Tsushima.*
Boston: Little, Brown & Company, 1911.

HANSON, HALDORE. *Humane Endeavour.* New York:
Farrar and Rinehart, Inc., 1939.

HEINL, ROBERT D. *Dictionary of Military and Naval Quotations.*
Annapolis: The Naval Institute, 1966.

HUGHES, NATHANIEL CHEAIRS, JR. *General William J. Hardee—
Old Reliable.* Baton Rouge: Louisiana State
University Press, 1965.

HUNT, FRAZIER. *The Untold Story of Douglas MacArthur.*
New York: Devon-Adair, 1954.

HUTCHINSON, ELIOT D. *How to Think Creatively.* New York:
Abingdon, 1949.

JAMES, WILLIAM. *Pluralistic Universe.* New York and London:
Longman's, 1909.

JENNINGS, EUGENE E. *Anatomy of Leadership.* New York:
Harper & Row, 1960.

JOMINI, ANTOINE HENRI. *Art of War.* Edited by J. D. Hittle.
Harrisburg, Pa.: Stackpole, 1952.

KOESTLER, ARTHUR. *The Act of Creation.* New York:
Macmillan Company, 1964.

LAMB, HAROLD. *Hannibal.* New York:
Doubleday & Company, 1958.

LAWRENCE, T. E. *The Seven Pillars of Wisdom.* New York:
Doubleday & Company, 1947.

LEE, CLARK AND RICHARD HENSCHEL. *Douglas MacArthur.*
New York: Henry Holt, 1952.

LIDDELL HART, B. H. *T. E. Lawrence.* London:
Jonathan Cape, 1934.

LOCKWOOD, CHARLES A. AND HANS CHRISTIAN ADAMSON. *Through
Hell and Deep Water.* New York: Chilton, 1956.

LUDWIG, EMIL. *Napoleon.* New York: Boní & Liveright, 1926.

MACHIAVELLI, NICCOLÒ DE BERNARDO. *The Art of War.*
Albany, N. Y.: H. C. Southwick, 1815.

MAHAN, ALFRED THAYER. *Admiral Farragut.* New York:
Appleton & Company, 1892.

————— . *The Influence of Sea Power upon History, 1660 to 1783.* Boston: Little, Brown & Company, 1918.

————— . *Life of Nelson.* Boston: Little, Brown & Company, 1918.

————— . *Naval Strategy.* Boston: Little, Brown & Company, 1911.

————— . *Types of Naval Officers.* Boston: Little, Brown & Company, 1918.

MALTZ, MAXWELL. *Psycho-Cybernetics.* Englewood Cliffs, N. J.: Prentice-Hall, 1960.

MAO TSE-TUNG. *On Guerrilla Warfare.* Translated by Samuel B. Griffith. New York: Frederick A. Praeger, 1961.

MAUGHAM, W. SOMERSET. *The Summing Up.* New York: Doubleday & Company, 1938.

MONSARRAT, NICHOLAS. *The Cruel Sea.* New York: Alfred A. Knopf, Inc., 1951.

MONTGOMERY, BERNARD LAW (Viscount Montgomery of Alamein). *The Path to Leadership.* New York: G. P. Putnam's Sons, 1961.

MORISON, SAMUEL ELIOT. *History of United States Naval Operations in World War II—New Guinea and the Marianas, March 1944-August 1944, Vol. VIII.* Boston: Little, Brown & Company, 1960.

————— . *John Paul Jones.* Boston: Little, Brown & Company, 1959.

MORRIS, DONALD R. *Washing of the Spears.* New York: Simon & Schuster, 1965.

NEY, VIRGIL. *Notes on Guerrilla Warfare.* Washington, D.C.: Command Publications, 1961.

OGILVY, DAVID. *Confessions of an Advertising Man.* New York: Atheneum, 1963.

OSBORN, ALEX F. *Applied Imagination.* New York: Charles Scribner's Sons, 1963.

PAYNE, ROBERT. *Mao Tse-tung, Ruler of Red China.* New York: Henry Schuman, 1950.

POTTER, E. P. AND CHESTER W. NIMITZ, eds., *Sea Power: A Naval History*. Englewood Cliffs, N.J.: Prentice-Hall, 1960.

PULESTON, WILLIAM D. MAHAN. *The Life and Works of Captain Alfred Thayer Mahan, U.S.N.* New Haven: Yale University Press, 1939.

RAUDSEPP, EUGENE. *Managing Creative Scientists and Engineers.* New York: Macmillan Company, 1963.

ROBISON, S. S. AND MARY L. ROBISON. *A History of Naval Tactics from 1530 to 1930.* Annapolis: U.S. Naval Institute, 1942.

ROSCOE, THEODORE. *United States Submarine Operations in World War II.* Annapolis: U.S. Naval Institute, 1949.

SAXE, MAURICE DE. *Reveries on the Art of War.* Translated by T. R. Phillips. Harrisburg, Pa.: Military Service Publishing Company, 1947.

SCOTT, ROBERT LEE. *Flying Tiger.* New York: Doubleday & Company, 1959.

SUN TZU. *The Art of War.* Translated by Lionel Giles. Harrisburg, Pa.: Military Service Publishing Company, 1944.

TAYLOR, THEODORE. *The Magnificent Mitscher.* New York: Norton & Company, 1954.

THAYER, CHARLES W. *Guerrilla.* New York: Harper & Row, 1963.

THURSFIELD, JAMES R. *Nelson and Other Naval Studies.* New York: E. P. Dutton, 1920.

TOLSTOI, LEV NIKOLAEVICH. *What Is Art?* Translated by Aylmer Maude. London: Oxford Press (World's Classics), 1959.

WARD, JAMES H. *Manual of Naval Tactics.* New York: D. von Nostrand & Company, 1859.

WAVELL, ARCHIBALD PERCIVAL. *Soldiers and Soldiering.* London: Jonathan Cape, 1953.

WESCOTT, ALLEN. *Mahan on Naval Warfare.* London: Sampson Low, Marston & Co., Ltd., 1919.

WILKINSON, BURKE. *By Sea and By Stealth.* New York: Coward-McCann, Inc., 1965.

WILLOUGHBY, CHARLES A. AND JOHN CHAMBERLAIN. *MacArthur, 1941-1951.* New York: McGraw-Hill Book Company, 1954.

WYETH, JOHN A. *That Devil Forrest*. New York: Harper & Brothers, 1959.

YOUNG, DESMOND. *Rommel, The Desert Fox*. New York: Harper & Brothers, 1950.

ARTICLES

ADAMS, T. W. "Creativity Conflict: Management versus Scientists," *Army Research and Development Newsmagazine*, August 1963, IV, 1, p. 30.

BARR, ALFRED H. JR. *What Is Modern Painting?* Garden City: The Museum of Modern Art, 1956.

BARRON, FRANK. "The Psychology of Imagination," *Scientific American*, September, 1958, CIC, p. 164.

BRADLEY, OMAR N. "Leadership," *Military Review*, September 1966, pp. 48-53.

BUCKNELL, HOWARD. "Give of Yourself, Captain," U.S. Naval Institute *Proceedings*, Vol. 90, No. 6, June 1964, p. 73.

DRURY, MICHAEL. "Of Course You're Creative!" *Glamour*, February 1959, p. 91.

GRIGG, WILLIAM. "That Headstrong Kid Is Geared to Succeed," Washington *Evening Star*, May 5, 1946, p. A-1.

"Lincoln and Modern America," *Time*. May 10, 1963, p. 20.

McPHERSON, J. H. "The Creative Patent Attorney," *Journal of the Patent Office Society*, XLVI, No. 4, April 1964, pp. 292-300.

MOFFITT, DONALD A. "Maverick Managers," *The Wall Street Journal*, Vol. XXVIII (November 22, 1961), No. 101, pp. 1, 8.

MORGAN, WILLIAM J. "The Pivot Upon Which Everything Turned," *The Iron Worker*, Spring 1958.

MOUROMTSEFF, I. E. "Who Is the True Inventor?" *Institute of Radio Engineers Proceedings*, June 1950.

MRAZEK, JAMES E., "The Creativity of the Guerrilla," *Army*, June 1964, pp. 86-90.

———— . "War As an Art," U.S. Naval Institute *Proceedings*, Vol. 89, No. 3, March 1963, pp. 66-71.

———— . "Submarine Captain, A Study in Intellectual Creativity," *Navy*, January 1965.

———— . "Rembrandts of the Military Art," *Army,*
January 1965, pp. 63-67.

———— . "Battle Creativity for the Staff," *Military Review,*
December 1965, pp. 22-26.

———— . "The Philosophy of the Guerrilla Fighter,"
The Army Quarterly and Defense Journal, London:
April 1968, pp. 64-67.

———— . "The Philosophy of the Guerrilla Fighter," *The Army
Quarterly and Defense Journal,* London: April 1968, pp. 64-67.

NITZE, PAUL. "Brains in the Navy," *The Washington Post,* June
1, 1964, p. A-18.

OSBORN, ALEX F. *Developments in the Creative Education
Movement,* based on an address at the 8th Annual Creative
Problem Solving Institute at the University of Buffalo, p. 1.

PARLOFF, MORRIS B. AND JOSEPH H. HANDLON. "The Influence of
Criticalness on Creative Problem Solving in Dyads," *Psychiatry,*
February 1, 1964, pp. 17-27.

PIAO, LIN. "Lin Piao's Manifesto," *Army,* December 1965,
pp. 47-51, taken from the Red Chinese *Peking Review,*
No. 36, September 3, 1965, compiled and condensed by
Dr. Fritz G. A. Kreamer for *Army.*

RIDGWAY, MATTHEW B. "Leadership," *Military Review,*
October 1966, pp. 40-49.

TAYLOR, MAXWELL. "Some Reflections on the Subject of
Leadership," from an address to students, the Citadel, 1956,
taken from *Military Leadership,* West Point: United States
Military Academy, 1960, p. 90.

WATSON, MARK S. "Control of the Military," *Ordnance,*
November-December 1962, p. 289.

YASYUKOV, M. "Soviet Armed Forces Place Special Emphasis on
Initiative and Ingenuity," (*Navy* title and translated from an
article by Lt. Col. M. Yasyukov in *Kommunist Voorushennykh
Sil,* Moscow, no date or page given by *Navy*), *Navy,*
December 1963, p. 36.

REPORTS

BURKE, ARLIEGH A. "Interview of Commander Arliegh A. Burke

U.S.N. on the Battle of Empress of Augustus Bay,"
July 31, 1945, Number 411-1, Washington, D.C.: Office of the
Chief of Naval History, p. 20.

————— . "Action Report of Night Engagement off Cape Moltke
on Night of November 1st-2nd, 1943," COMDESRON 23,
Serial 012, November 1943, Washington: Office of the
Chief of Naval History, p. 29.

CTF (Command Task Force) 58 (Vice Admiral Mitscher)
Action Report, September 11, 1944 (Washington, D.C.: Office
of the Chief of Naval History), p. 27.

DEALEY, S. D. *Report of War Patrol Number Three—U.S.S.
HARDER*, Washington, D.C.: Office of the Chief of Naval
History, p. 8.

HARDING, HAROLD F. "Place of Creativity in the Military Mission,"
Military Creative Problem Solving Seminar, Fort Belvoir:
U.S. Army Management School, March 1961. p. 53.

MAURER, J. H. *Report of War Patrol Number One —
U.S.S. ATULE (SS403)*. Report SS403/A16/ASerial 013,
Arlington, Va.: Office of the Chief of Naval History,
December 11, 1944.

Military Leadership Situational Studies. West Point, N.Y.:
2nd ed. 1960.

RENDULIC, LOTHAR. "The Command Decision." Unpublished
manuscript originally prepared for Headquarters, European
Command, Office of the Chief Historian (1947) and later
printed by the Office of the Chief of Military History, Department of the Army and issued as background material to deci-
sion-making studies conducted by students at the Command
and General Staff College of the Army, Fort Leavenworth,
Kansas, April 8, 1958.

U.S.S. Enterprise Reports of July 3, 1944 (Washington, D.C.:
Office of the Chief of Naval History), p. 340.

OTHER SOURCES

KOCH, OSCAR. Letter to Colonel Mrazek, June 17, 1968.

MAURER, J. H. Personal interview conducted at the Pentagon,
Washington, D.C.: May 8, 1964.

Index